Twitter Revolution

How Social Media and Mobile Marketing is Changing the Way We Do Business & Market Online

Deborah Micek & Warren Whitlock

AKA:

@CoachDeb & @WarrenWhitlock

Legal Notice:

While all attempts have been made to verify information provided in this publication, neither the Author nor the Publisher assumes any responsibility for errors, omissions, or contrary interpretation of the subject matter herein.

This publication is not intended for use as a source of legal or accounting advice. The Publisher wants to stress that the information contained herein may be subject to varying state and/or local laws or regulations. All users are advised to retain competent counsel to determine what state and/or local laws or regulations may apply to the user's particular business.

The purchaser or reader of this publication assumes responsibility for the use of these materials and information. Adherence to all applicable laws and regulations, federal, state, and local, governing professional licensing, business practices, advertising, and all other aspects of doing business in the United States or any other jurisdiction is the sole responsibility of the purchaser or reader.

The author and Publisher assume no responsibility or liability whatsoever on behalf of any purchaser or reader of these materials. Any perceived slights of specific people or organizations are unintentional.

Library of Congress Cataloging in-Publication Data:
Micek, Deborah and Whitlock, Warren

TWITTER REVOLUTION: How social media and mobile marketing is changing the way we do business & market online

p.   cm.

ISBN 978-1-934275-07-8 and 1-934275-07-7
1. **Marketing**   2. **Business Blogging**   3. **Social Media**

Printed and bound in the United States of America.

Published by:

Xeno Press
6130 W Flamingo #231
Las Vegas NV 89103
702-953-5843

DEDICATION

This book was created for and with all the early adopters of micro-blogging and social networks who were part of the world's largest and longest cocktail party on Twitter when it was at its most exciting apex; thanks for all your contribution and participation in helping to make this a revolutionary book – the 1st one of its kind.

Visit the Online book to see the early adopter tweeters who contributed to the writing of this book at: http://TwitterHandbook.com/blog

You Rock!

DISCLOSURE:

Twitter Revolution is a living book that will change and continue to evolve with your participation and community interaction online.

Participate in this community and LIVING document where YOU can give us your feedback in the online at:

TwitterHandbook.com

NO RULES

The revolution is underway. The power of social media lies with the people who use tools like Twitter.com. You decide how to use your power.

Our goal is *not* to create rules to follow on Twitter. We simply want to give you the best tips, resources and strategies to guide your success on Twitter at an accelerated pace.

Our mission is to help you avoid trial and error as early adopters were forced to endure, and help you participate in one of the greatest communication revolution of our time.

This book was designed to help show everyone from the small business owner to the CEO of a large corporation; from work at home moms to politicians in Washington, DC how they can participate in the fastest growing social network and micro-blogging revolution taking place right now.

Join us on Twitter!

Rave Reviews

BlogSquad @CoachDeb The Twitter Handbook is going to be required reading for all Blog Squad clients. Posted my review on TTH blog 38 minutes ago

DonnaFox @WarrenWhitlock amazes me every day. Spend time with him if you get the rare opportunity. He knows things that will make your head spin! 8 minutes ago

MichaelDWalker Twitter Revolution is a fast, informative guide that shows you how to utilize the social revolution's new leader in concise communication about 5 hours ago

bgreen still in awe about how comprehensive Twitter Revolution by @CoachDeb & @WarrenWhitlock is, changing people's lives 1 tweet at a time :~) 18 minutes ago

jimkukral @coachdeb and @warrenwhitlock take Twitter and make it understandable for non-Internet geeks. Their book is a much needed guide for an extremely powerful tool that all businesses need to get on board with. About 7 minutes ago

douglaslampi @coachdeb Reading the pre-release version of Twitter Revolution with WIDE eyes! I never thought that far ahead about business use of Twitter! About 11 hours ago

GrantGriffiths Have I told you that the book is freaking awesome. WOW. Seriously, this is a great tool for someone to use to get a jump start with twitter about 9 hours ago

InitheLivingRoom @coachdeb the Twitter Revolution is full of new ideas for using Twitter. It is a must read for everyone new and old. I can't stop reading it about 6 hours ago

allaboutenergy @CoachDeb Just completed Twitter Revolution! I LUV IT! Better than I could have ever imagined! U and @WarrenWhitlock did a Twitabulous Job! About 2 hours ago

barefoot_exec @CoachDeb @warrenwhitlock – just posted review of TwitterRev – wow – NICELY done! I'm a BELIEVER! 38 minutes ago

BenMack @coachdeb How Social Media and Mobile Media are Changing the Way We do Business & Marketing Online in 140 CHARACTERS OR LESS about 9 hours ago

bestreflections @CoachDeb and @WarrenWhitlock finished Twitter Revolution. Education is a better word.. a gift! A wealth of info Links alone r gold. About 11 hours ago

coacheva @CoachDeb Ya doin' an OUTRAGEOUSLY OUTSTANDING JOB on da book. Lovin' u and @warrenwhitlock – in HUGE appreciation about 6 hours ago

michelletrent @CoachDeb What a Book! Thank U 4 giving me the opportunity to preview & leave comments on Twitter Revolution! The ULTIMATE Guide to twitter! About 5 hours ago

marykw @CoachDeb and @WarrenWhitlock Twitter Revolution – defining the indefinable! A read worth it's followers in GOLD! LOVE the Bonus Tips! About 9 hours ago

mediastarr HUGE fan of the Matrix now even BIGGER fan of Twitter when @WarrenWhitlock turned me on 2 it, I had no idea how it would chng my biz & life! 4 minutes ago

MichDdot deb I am amzed serious, im looking at your book as a man with 20+ years of sales marketing and conceptual advertising exp. HOLY S#!T about 3 hours ago

davidbullock @CoachDeb @WarrenWhitlock "THE" Twitter Revolution is awesome. Just left you a comment. My tweets will not be the same thx a bunch 2 minutes ago

deborahcarraro @CoachDeb Congrats! Book is G8! Can't wait to tell world about it! about 9 hours ago

FeliciaSlattery @CoachDeb I'm reading it now. Twitter Revolutions is awesome. Can't wait til it's ready to share w/ my peeps who keep asking why the fuss about 7 hours ago

fitnessbyphone @CoachDeb I enjoyed pre-release copy of Twitter Revolution amputting it to use already – the future is business relationships between PEOPLE 44 minutes ago

KatieDarden @CoachDeb Build relationships, discover nu resources, make money & have fun- that's Twitter ina nutshell& TwRevolution helps u make the most of it! About 3hours ago

keithdb @CoachDeb The Twitter Revolution is good stuff... love the twitter apps—more ways to play! About 9 hours ago

LifeCoachKaren @CoachDeb LUVD it!!! Invaluable. @BookWarren reminded me 2 post on blog http://TwitterHandbook.com/... So here I go :~) about 7 hours ago

LisaVanAllen @CoachDeb Just sent an email for the pw for the handbook!! Thx for a gr8 call! Gr8 content – as always! You rock! 20 minutes ago

ResPres @CoachDeb @WarrenWhitlock Just finished first quick read of pre-rel Twitter Revolutions – Well Done! about 9 hours ago

MandoFierro @coachdeb and @warrenwhitlock Twitter Revolution rocks! I'm encouraging all my tweeps to get a copy when it comes out! 5 minutes ago

MarieLCoccia @CoachDeb @BookWarren Sneakin' my peak at life-changing Twitter Revolution pre-release http://twitterhandbook.com about 3 hours ago

markress The "GURUS" say Twitter is a waste of time.. 3 & a half mnths & ovr $75k later I say WHATEVER. If you help ppl & provide value U WILL make $$ 28 minutes ago

nancymk @CoachDeb as always you are doing a great job. Keep it up. We appreciate you! 21 minutes ago

PamRagland @CoachDeb @WarrenWhitlock Just finished pre-rel Twitter Revolution-Awesome! This is a guide to the new millennium, not just Twitter about 14 hours ago

ericfarewell @CoachDeb rocks my world.. And summarily, should rock yours as well… follow her and prepare to be rocked (in a good way) about 5 hours ago

Deremiah_CPE @warrenwhitlock @coachdeb come on with the product… I need to move 5,000 lbs of Twitter books on the streets. My peeps need this one about 10 hours ago

wwhitlock Twitter Revolution intro is a masterful summation of the place New Media Revolution in the flow of human desire to be understood about 8 hours ago

SharonMcP @CoachDeb http://twitpic.com9jan – The power of Twitter never stops amazing me. #Twitcast 17 minutes ago

TedChan @CoachDeb just finished most recent twitcast. Re-learned: be loved or hated but never tolerated. Build a tribe of fans 19 minutes ago

Table of Contents

PART THREE:

*Influence & Persuasion
to position & brand yourself on
Twitter & other social networks*

PART FOUR:

*iChapters
The Twitter Playbook*

Foreword

By Robert Scoble AKA: @Scobleizer
Author of *Naked Conversations How Blogs Are Changing the Way Businesses Talk With Customers*

Last night I watched Twitter during the Republican National Convention.

Many people don't understand what I just said.

First, most people have never seen Twitter. This book introduces Twitter to you in all of its glory and all of its noisy nonsense too.

But what do I mean by "watching Twitter?"

Well, you can use a tool like Twitter Vision http://www.twittervision.com to watch people around the world Tweet. Er, post things into Twitter.

Or, as I was doing last night, I was using one of the real-time search engines that let me watch what people are writing about in real time.

The two most popular are FriendFeed's search engine and Twitter's search engine. These are remarkable because they let you search - in live time.
Why is this important?

Well, remember the Chinese earthquake in 2008? I was on Twitter that night using Twhirl to watch what my friends were talking about. Within a few minutes several people said "just felt an earthquake." Then I started using the search engines to see what other Twitter users had said. In just the first two minutes - before the USGS Website had even confirmed the earthquake and 45 minutes before CNN talked about it - I saw several people in several different cities who had talked about the earthquake. I knew then that it was a major seismic event and, sure enough, over the next three hours the news came flooding in. Some people posted URLs to the first news reports in the New York Times or CNN. Others posted video or photos their friends had shot. And other people came online to give their personal experiences.

This is now like talk radio where we can hear experiences of everyday people. With one difference. This is a World Wide Talk Show. And thanks to URLs and the rest of the Web it isn't just words, either.

It's amazing to look back at what was launched with a blogging tool that limited you to 140 characters. I remember the first reactions that many of my readers had when I first tried to tell them about Twitter.

"It's lame" is one reaction that sticks in my head. After all, if you don't have any friends on Twitter and you see people talking about what they had for lunch you can easily draw that conclusion on first look.

But the experiences I've had, along with many other people, on Twitter, show that it's far from the simplistic "it's lame" first impression. There's companies, like Zappos or Dell on Twitter. I'll never forget doing my taxes in HR Block and getting a Tweet from an HR Block employee who was working thousands of miles away. There's fire departments, like Los Angeles, who are using Twitter to report what their department is responding to. There are political candidates, or their staffs anyway, who are using it to push info out but I've met two Congressmen who actually are using Twitter themselves.

In this book you'll hear all about that, and much more. Enjoy your foray into this new world of communications and I'll see you @scobleizer on Twitter.

Follow Robert Scoble on Twitter @Scobleizer and get one of the most popular blogs online at: http://Scobleizer.com

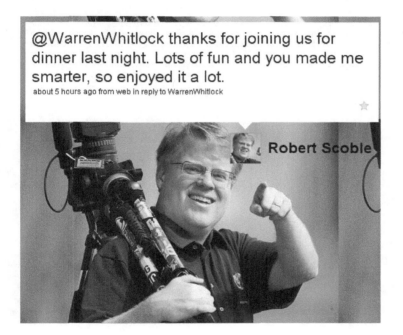

WARNING:

What you're about to open is NOT your typical book.

It is NOT for everyone.
It may cause serious disturbance to your psyche.

If you did not like e.e. cummings, the poet who rebelled against the rules by refusing to use capitalization or traditional English rules, you will NOT like this book either. It's full of tweets from people who use creative spelling in order to get their point across in 140 characters or less.

If you judge a book based on its proper use of the English language, you will NOT like this book.

> WARNING Put this book down if U R stickler 4 spelling & grammar=It's full of tweets & tribal twitter lingo that may disturb English teacher
> 2 minutes ago from web
>
> Deborah Micek

This book is as revolutionary as the social media revolution taking place this very moment in the way people communicate.

Twitter is all about SPEED and PARTICIPATING in the CONVERSATION. Its members consist of the brightest minds, trendsetters, early adopters and innovators in tech, Web 3.0, and business professionals. These people know how to see the future use of a tool and become first in their field to use it.

The biggest challenge of any Tweeter is fitting your message in 140 characters or less. Sometimes, that requires altering the English language in order to complete the tweet.

Sometimes, it requires being an original thinker as to how you can still say the same thing, just slightly different by taking OUT some filler words that you discover are rather unnecessary.

As with any type of tool that's on the bleeding edge and very new to the world, the level of acceptance for the tool in the mind of each individual user will be determined by asking yourself one question—what types of opportunities or dangers do *you* see in using it?

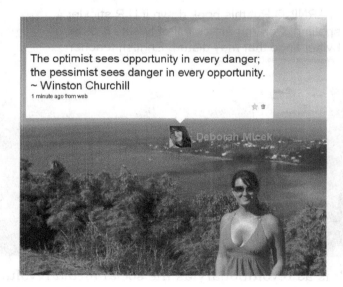

The optimist sees opportunity in every danger; the pessimist sees danger in every opportunity.
~ Winston Churchill
1 minute ago from web

Preface

Even though Twitter has its up and down times, we tend to stay with it like a bad boyfriend. Why is that? Twitter has both a tribal and seductive quality about it that makes it more addicting than cocaine.

An Ode to Twitter:
How do I love thee?
Let me count the ways...

By @CoachDeb

If **Elizabeth Barrett Browning** (1806–1861) were alive to experience the Twit experience, I think she'd write something like this...

Twitter, how do I love thee? Let me count the ways...

1 1,000, 2 1,000... I love thee to the depth and breadth and height my tweet can reach.

When feeling out of sight, I use Jott to speak my love for thee.

I love thee to the level of everyday's most quiet need. By sun and candlelight, but best of all, by my battery plugged-in iPhone so I'm never out of touch.

I love thee when I'm lonely; I love thee when I'm busy; I love thee when I'm waiting in line. How you help me pass the time.

Twitter, how do I love thee? Let me count the ways. I love thee when I'm eating; I love thee when I'm sleeping; but I especially love thee when I'm tweeting.

I love thee freely, as I bring Jott, Twummize and Twemes together for ideal grace.

I love thee purely, as I get all my thoughts @ exactly 140 characters.

I love thee with a passion put to use as my follower count increases.

I love thee with a love I seem to lose when feeling out of touch with the rest of the world while shut up in my office.

And if the whale doth choose, I shall but love thee better after death.

(Or I'll just use Twiddict.com until you're back again for instant, quick tweeting.)

Introduction to Social Media

By Deborah Micek & John-Paul Micek

This INTRO was taken (with permission) directly from Chapter 1 of *Secrets of Online Persuasion* by Deborah Micek & John-Paul Micek, AKA: @DeborahMicek & @JPmicek authors of the first published book on New Media Marketing. You can get your own copy at: http://snipurl.com/SOPhardcover

[If you've already read that book, you can skip this intro and go directly to GO—er, I mean Chapter 1 of this book. ☺ We only added 2 things, but you'll notice them in the "Tweet-like bubbles" on the following pages.]

The New Media Revolution

The tidal wave of cultural transformation is not coming. It has already hit.

"They are the gatekeepers. They are guarding all the doors and they are holding all the keys, which means that sooner or later someone is going to have to fight them.

I won't lie to you Neo. Every single man or woman who has stood their ground, everyone who has fought an agent has died. But where they have failed, you will succeed.

I've seen an agent punch through a concrete wall; men have emptied entire clips at them and hit nothing but air. Yet their strength and their power is still based in a world that is built on rules. Because of that they will never be as strong or as fast as you can be."

Morpheus to Neo in the movie The Matrix

Most people are missing it, and that's good...for you. Because now, with the help of what we'll be sharing with you in this book, **you'll see opportunities** where your competitors and peers feel confusion and frustration.

What's the mistake? What are people missing? It's the tidal wave of cultural transformation that's sweeping the modern marketplace—a Revolution that's happening offline, online, and everywhere in between.

It's easy to miss. Since this reformation of the marketplace is being powered by the New Media, it looks like it's all about technology. And that intimidates most people. But don't allow yourself to be fooled. It's not about the Internet, blogs, iPods, or any other cool new tool on its own.

People, participation, and persuasion are generating the Revolution.

That concept is so important to your business success in the marketplace of the new millennium that it bears repeating. The New Media Revolution is about *people, participation, and persuasion.*

Grasp this one concept and you'll quickly leapfrog your competitors to lead your niche in marketing, buzz, and branding.

As Seth Godin first forecasted in his 1999 book *Permission Marketing*, traditional advertising and marketing through interruption is dead. Today, despite the companies large and small who still blindly stumble along, following habitual patterns of the past, the new millennium consumer has proved Seth's forecast to be true.

Will you follow in those same old footsteps until the reality of failure hits you? Or will you ignore the lie that others are telling themselves and profit from this exciting new marketplace?

The Lie We've All Been Living

When looking at what's happening in the marketplace, especially New Media, many people, including industry experts and experienced consultants, are focused on the "new" technologies of the New Media. Many more are caught up with a focus on the "media" of blogs, podcasts, social networks, and other New Media tools.

Keep in mind, it's not about the newness of technology and tools. The cultural transformation we're experiencing is certainly enabled by New Media. Yet if you're going to quickly adapt and profit in this new marketplace, it's critical to understand that this Revolution is a much deeper, cultural event. It's about returning to what drives us as human beings.

This is easy to see when we look at 8,000 years of recorded history. What's happened to marketing and communications over the last 80 years is an anomaly—a departure from what's natural for human beings.

From the birth of Christ, through the golden age of Islam at the end of the first millennium, the creation of the Gutenberg press in 1440, to the American Revolution in 1776 and beyond—the universal hunger has always been for freedom, connection, and participation. With each transformational period in history, people have been drawn to what empowers them and enhances what makes human beings human.

The latest interruption to that drive for freedom, connection, and participation began in the 1920s with the emergence of the first radio and television stations. It was harmless enough at first. Even helpful to bring people together as families gathered together in the living room to watch *I Love Lucy*.

But from the very start, the mindset of the Industrial Revolution was intertwined with mass media. Mass production and mass distribution permeated every area of the marketplace, and for nearly three quarters of a century that methodology continued to expand like a cancerous growth throughout mass media.

The lie spread (that this one-way channel is THE way to connect with people) and became so much a part of our lives that we didn't even stop to see it for what it really was.

Then, like many times before in history, the Revolution began.

The Ripples that Became a Tsunami

Like a series of earthquakes occurring in the middle of the ocean, deep on the sea floor, it went mostly unnoticed.

- The emergence of popular talk radio in 1989.

- The information superhighway of the Internet in the early 1990s.

- Lightning-fast viral communication through online social networks and blogs in the early years of the new millennium.

- Tools and media that put the customer in control like blogs, iPods, and podcasts.

As these and many other events occurred, it was much like the ocean waters draining away from the shoreline signaling an impending tsunami.

Early in the new millennium came the dethroning of Dan Rather, Trent Lott, and the New York Times—all due to stupid comments or falsified news. All of them were exposed by the New Media. With those events, a series of tidal waves struck. The very foundations of the news industry and politics were shaken to their core.

But the difference with this New Media tsunami is that the water hasn't receded. The New Media Revolution, first felt in the arenas of politics and news, is now sweeping through the entire culture. This Revolution is transforming everything in its path—including the customers and the marketplace you rely on for your success.

The Revolution is Not New

In 1440, Johannes Gutenberg also ignited a revolution. He did it by inventing a printing press—later called a movable type press. (So named as a result of the technology that allowed wood or metal letters to be moved on the printing plates.)

The main purpose of that technology was to mass reproduce Bibles, which up until that point were only printed in Latin. Since the majority of the public could only read their native language, while others could not read at all, the elite had to "reveal" the Scriptures to the public.

In just over half a century, the Revolution fueled by this one technology reached a flashpoint. Martin Luther nailed his 95 Theses on the door of the Castle Church in Wittenberg, Germany, in 1517. These documents dispelled the power and efficacy of indulgences and initiated a reformation of the power structure within the Catholic Church. With indulgences, bishops were playing God by selling forgiveness of sins.

The Revolution may have begun with Bibles, but very quickly, books of all kinds began to be translated, duplicated, and spread around the world at a rapid rate. This put information into the hands of common people instead of it being reserved for the elite.

Today, similar to Gutenberg's printing press, New Media is wrestling power and control of information from the elite once again.

New Media is turning mass media on its head. New Media is personal and participatory. It's about conversations rather than lectures. Information isn't being handed down from on high as if it's the Holy Scriptures anymore.

During the time of Gutenberg and Martin Luther you could say that the printers, publishers and writers were intellectual capitalists. They were using technology to transform the culture and were making a profit from that service.

Back then, the elites were the popes, kings, and lords who held the information and disseminated it to the masses as they saw fit.

Today, the intellectual capitalists are bloggers, talk radio hosts, podcasters, and now...Tweeters! Intellectual capitalists are the innovative business people savvy enough to recognize the transformation empowered by New Media, who then adapt and flow with the changes rather than fighting them.

Now, the elites range from the mass media to large corporations and the government. They are the monarchs of the modern day who are fighting tooth and nail to retain their base of power—the control and dissemination of information.

The Early Years of The New Media Revolution

If we go with the viewpoint that the New Media Revolution began in the early 1990s, then talk radio must be seen as one of the earliest "tremors" to be felt.

Talk radio took a traditional mass media form—radio—and turned it into something participatory.

While we wouldn't consider talk radio to be part of the New Media that business people need to focus on for growth and profits, it is important to understand why it's so popular.

Why is it that a host like Rush Limbaugh has 25 million people a day listening to his radio show? It's because compared to a regular radio show, it's participatory.

People want their voices to be heard. And they want to hear from other people who think like them. Whether they agree or disagree with the host, they want the opportunity to call up and speak their mind.

After the introduction of talk radio, the Internet entered the scene. As more and more people went online each year throughout the nineties, the New Media started taking shape.

The proliferation of broadband access made it possible for waves of change to move very quickly.

And now with services like Twitter that allow you to send messages to the masses from your mobile phone, the mass media can no longer silence the people.

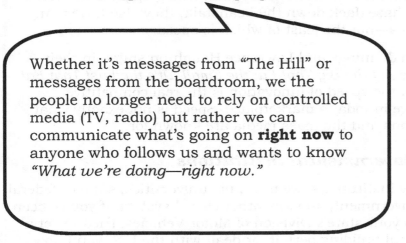

Whether it's messages from "The Hill" or messages from the boardroom, we the people no longer need to rely on controlled media (TV, radio) but rather we can communicate what's going on **right now** to anyone who follows us and wants to know *"What we're doing—right now."*

Today, the Revolution has irreversible momentum. Yet, not everyone likes what's happening.

The Gatekeepers and Guardians of The Status Quo

The New Media tsunami is thundering through the marketplace, transforming everything in its path. Now that you realize that the Revolution is about people, participation, and persuasion, it's time to share an even more important secret.

The secret is in the opportunity that entrepreneurs and small business owners have; an unprecedented growth opportunity like never before in history.

Why is there such opportunity? Because the institutions and power structures of the past are still unwilling to flex and flow with the transformation taking place.

The institutions that dominated the Industrial Era are having their power to control and influence the masses erode right before their very eyes!

Corporations, government, and mass media may seem like giants, but like the slumbering giant who groggily awoke and tried to chase Jack down the beanstalk, they also have many limitations—not the least of which is speed.

As Jason Jennings and Lawrence Haughton stated in their book, *It's Not the Big That Eat the Small...It's the Fast That Eat the Slow*, the speed of innovation is the real competitive advantage in today's marketplace. Speed is not exactly what institutions and the mass media are known for.

Governmental Institutions

By institutions, we mean big universities, state or federal government, and any other closed system. If you've been to your state's Division of Motor Vehicles, tried to get a local building permit, or dealt with the IRS, you know what we're talking about. You're dealing with a system that doesn't like to admit fallibility. A system where there's a long-standing hierarchy which seeks to protect itself.

Because of that, change (especially anything that appears to threaten existing hierarchies) is shunned as evil. Every possible effort is made to hide, minimize, or deride the truth of the transformational forces.

Corporations

Most corporations don't have a structure that allows for rapid adaptation. Many corporations today still operate based on the principles of the Industrial Revolution. They see employees as cogs in the machine, and consumers as a herd of unthinking animals ready to be sold as black and white solutions.

Even Internet industries, which are supposed to be "cutting edge", reveal their thinking through their actions.

Take broadband Internet access for example. Broadband infrastructure was built for fast downloads, not for uploads. Even if you have cable or DSL, you can download quickly, but it takes much longer to upload files.

Thanks to the mindset shaped by the mass media, mass marketing, and mass distribution, these corporations didn't see people putting back in as much as they took out. They didn't think about people participating.

Newspapers and Network Television

This is another group fighting the New Media Revolution. Readership and viewership are dropping precipitously.

Every month there are stories in the mass media about how readership is declining. Newsrooms across the country have let go of a huge percentage of their workforce over the last decade.

Why?

Because people are tired of being told what to think with no option to participate and share their two cents worth.

The credibility and power of major newspapers are being eroded, and it's the New Media that's chipping away at that.

Sure there was the New York Times scandal with Jayson Blair, and a host of others that expose the fallibility of mass media in news reporting. But take a look at the more practical side of mass media related to business.

For example, in every town that Craigslist (www.craigslist.com) enters, the local newspapers (large and small) shudder in fear because they know their advertising and classifieds are going to plummet.

Craigslist is instantly searchable, always up-to-date, and interactive. For both advertisers and prospective buyers, dead tree papers are inconvenient, expensive, and completely non-participatory.

These guardians of the past may fight hard to protect the status quo, but in doing so, they're leaving a tremendous void in the marketplace—a void that fast-moving entrepreneurs and business owners will fill and profit from, if they take action sooner rather than later.

The Shakeout and The Current Opportunity for Fast-Acting Movers

The shakeout between the fast and the slow has already begun. The slow will fail in their feeble attempts at preserving the old ways.

"I know now what you're trying to do, and I'm going to let them all know—on Twitter!" ~ Neo

It reminds me of Neo in *The Matrix* at the end of part one, when Neo gets on the phone and says to those controlling and manipulating what people see:

Ok, so Neo didn't say "on Twitter" but I bet he was thinking it!

Now with the New Media, there is an army of Neos—hundreds of millions of change agents. They are passionate

Go ahead and send a tweet 2 @CoachDeb if you think Neo was thinking about Twitter when he said that in Matrix.

about participating in the marketplace conversation and transformation. And that strikes fear in the hearts of the entrenched institutions.

What Does This Mean to You and Your Business?

It means it's no longer "business as usual." It means you can't market, sell, or manage the way you did even just three years ago.

It also means you can give yourself a tremendous competitive advantage when you understand the New Media Marketplace.

If you're in business and you're not already feeling these changes, you will soon enough. The New Media world of blogs, podcasts, social networks, wikis, and more are enabling participation and connection like never before in history. If you want a head start on your competitors, it's something you must get involved with **now**.

It's not that you have to become a New Media expert. You don't even need to blog, podcast, or tweet every day. What it does mean is that you need to be aware of the New Media Marketplace and keep track of it even if you're not actively participating in it just yet.

Otherwise you can count on this—you will be pummeled by the whitewater of the tsunami when it hits you.

So, what makes the New Media Marketplace different? Is it really changing the way we do business from here on out?

You be the judge. Let's check out this brave new world together...shall we?

Chapter 1

Why Should You Care About Twitter?

Who Cares about Twitter?!

I was enjoying a delicious breakfast in the VIP lounge of the presidential suite in Singapore before getting ready to start a long day presenting to an audience of 500 business owners and internet marketers eager to learn about marketing with new media.

As I shoved the bacon aside, deciding it wasn't worth it, something on the news in the corner of the lounge caught my eye.

It was the first time I heard the word "Twitter" on the news. It was described by the CNN journalist as "the newest micro-blogging tool to hit the internet." She defined it as a place where teenagers were posting what they were doing throughout the day, from the cereal they were eating to the movies they were watching.

I thought to myself, *"Heck no!"*

Feel free to replace YOUR first reaction here, and you'll understand exactly how I felt.

As I reflect back on the early morning of that spring day, learning about Twitter from the

NOTE 2 Reader: Actually, in the spirit of transparency, my response was much stronger to John-Paul, sitting across from me (eating his bacon). But in the spirit of keeping this handbook rated PG... ☺

mainstream, elite media while in a different country, I realized how news reporters really don't get Twitter nor report Twitter in the way a business owner would.

Elite media positioned Twitter as if it was just another silly tool that teens were using to discuss banal things such as what they were having for breakfast. They made it appear to be a waste of time.

But there was no talk about how this tool could be revolutionary in breaking news all over the world. No mention of how businesses could take advantage of the medium to get their message out to their clients directly on their cell phones. No mention of how quickly information could be spread in the blink of an eye through this new word-of-mouth communication channel.

Nothing except the silliest reason they could describe to frame the tool as something trivial in the minds of their viewers, in the hopes that "we the people" wouldn't figure out how to use it to report the real news of what was happening—with our governments or corporations.

After all, as a business owner, CEO or executive, who has the time to waste talking about the bacon you just shoved aside, or that you're getting butterflies in your stomach before you're about to go on stage? After all, there's no value in sharing things like that!

Or IS there?

At first, my justification for not joining Twitter was that I was a coach, there to teach my clients how to use adult channels of new media marketing.

I didn't want to waste my time or my client's time pointing out every little doo-dad or cool tool that happened to be "fun" to play with for the moment, but not serve as a useful business communication tool.

My partner and I had a rule as new media marketing strategists. And that rule was that any "cool new tool" had to pass the "marketing test." In other words, if the tool didn't bring new traffic, lead to new clients, or generate new revenue, it was a mere distraction and we didn't bother wasting our clients' valuable time by mentioning it.

"That's where I draw the line!" I justified to my partner over breakfast in Singapore.

"Blogs are fantastic. We know how much they've helped us get traffic to our website and get more clients. They're great for SEO and getting our message out quickly, but I'm NOT getting involved with this 'Twitter' thingy! That's just pushing it. It's just not something I could get into. I'm TOO busy."

(Sound Familiar?)

Well, that was over a year ago. Since then I've personally investigated the tool further, instead of just taking the opinion of some stuffy journalist who fears communication tools like Twitter, another form of blogging they originally tried to ignore, hoping it would go away. I've not only joined Twitter, participated and become a daily *"Tweeter," but I've subsequently become a *"TwitAholic."

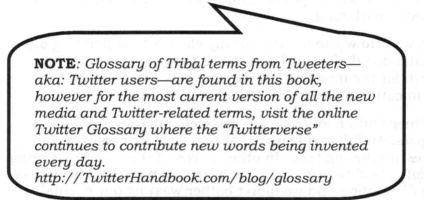

NOTE: *Glossary of Tribal terms from Tweeters— aka: Twitter users—are found in this book, however for the most current version of all the new media and Twitter-related terms, visit the online Twitter Glossary where the "Twitterverse" continues to contribute new words being invented every day.*
http://TwitterHandbook.com/blog/glossary

HEY! Don't laugh! Before the end of this book, if you don't get hooked on Twitter, you can laugh all you want.

WORD OF CAUTION: Be careful before you laugh at those using Twitter. Be even more careful what you say about not liking Twitter. And be extra careful about what you TWEET about your 1st impressions about Twitter.

This is stupid. I just signed up, but I don't see ever using this. I've got better things to do.

@name-withheld-to-protect-the-innocent

Because after all, all tweets become **permanent records** on the web that **cannot be deleted.** Dozens of internet marketers have already regretted blasting Twitter when they first joined. In fact, the majority of internet marketer's first tweets are usually something like:

I wound up becoming an early adopter. At first, I didn't use it that much. I just joined to grab my name and lock it up.

I would encourage you to at least lock up your name (if it's not gone already) as soon as you're finished reading this chapter, even if you're still on the fence about it.

> **Twitter Tip:** Register your Twitter name without the use of spaces or underscores. Many reasons why but the main reason is that underscores are a dead give away that you're a late adopter. *(It's also an extreme pain in the buttocks to get to the underscore when you're tweeting from an iPhone with no copy/paste feature.)*

Coach Deb

I've been on Twitter for 365+ days at the time of this writing, but have only actively used it for the past three to five months. I don't want anyone to feel late to the game because you can still be an early adopter if you join Twitter today. *(And when I say "today" I actually mean today…the day I'm writing this book.)*

Remember: Twitter is not the ONLY social media tool. It's just one of the HOTTEST places to be *right now* and where the brightest minds are hanging out. It's kind of like THE party to be at.

Twitter is only the beginning. Twitter started the social media revolution (some would say frenzy). But it won't be the last.

In fact, as I write this, there are developers working on an open source API that will be similar to Twitter, but the code will be available to ALL.

We'll keep our subscribers updated on all the new social media tools coming out via the blog @ http://TwitterHandbook.com

NOTE: Subscribers will also get bonus audios and reports to supplement what could not fit in this book, or what the editors deleted.

Join the *Twibe. Enjoy the journey. Welcome to the Twitterverse.

Twibe = your first lesson in deciphering Twitter-speak.

Twibe = Twitter Tribe

Laugh now. But by the end of this book, you'll be tweeting new words you create, as your brain starts thinking innovatively, and creatively.

Are you ready?

Chapter 2

What the Heck is Twitter?

How Do You Define Twitter?

Aye, there is the rub. Trying to define Twitter is like trying to define a shifting cultural trend. It's constantly morphing, changing, and adapting to YOU, the Twitter user, to be whatever YOU want it to be.

Originally Evan Williams, Twitter's founder, created it as a basic site to answer one simple question:

But it turned into SO much more than that.

The beauty of Twitter is that you do NOT have to answer that question every time you tweet.

In fact, it's better if you don't.

Be creative. Use Twitter as YOU see fit, and how it works for YOUR needs. We'll focus more on this in a future chapter.

For now, let's keep it simple for the Twitter newbie just hearing about Twitter and feeling much like I did on an early spring morning in Singapore.

We want to turn you on to the power that is Twitter.

Keep your mind open, and your brain thinking creatively.

Allow your heart to guide you to new ideas that have yet to be thought of.

Be the trend setter. Create something new with the tool that is Twitter.

What are YOU doing?

garygraye "No matter how small and unimportant what we are doing may seem, if we do it well, it may soon become the step that will lead us to better things." Channing Pollock Actor, Writer and Composer about 1 hour ago reply

What IS Twitter?

That is the question of the day, isn't it?

You've been hearing all this chatter about Twitter, perhaps you've even signed up, but then you're asking, *"Now what?!"* Right?! LOL (C'mon! Admit it! Even if you're a Twitterati by now, at one point, we all asked that question—right?)

When Coach Deb started actively tweeting (that's what they call it when you post on Twitter) she started describing Twitter by saying:

After laughs from a non-tweetin' partner, she asked her followers (AKA friends/fans) what they thought Twitter was through a post on the TwitterHandbook.com blog.

"Please share **your answer** in the comments below in 140 characters (give or take) for possible inclusion in the 1st published book on Twitter: Twitter Handbook. "

The blog post was as simple as that. No long-winded, detailed stories about what twitter is coming from some expert guru from on high. Instead, it was left "open-ended" with a question for all readers to answer.

(TIP: This is a KILLER coaching tip I'm giving you if you want to drive more traffic and conversations to your blog. Don't try to put everything in your own post. Let your readers be the expert. Give them the credit to offer insight and brilliance to the post.)

The following is what came back as replies within seconds of asking this question on Twitter.

First, we'll share the screen shot of the search feature that's now part of Twitter. Then we'll show you how it looks in the replies tab.

> **TWITTER TIP:** The tool to use to keep track of who is talking @ you whether they use the @ symbol in front of your name, or use it anywhere in the tweet (which you won't see in your replies tab) is formerly known as Summize.com (very short and easy to say and tweet). But now that Summize.com was bought out by Twitter, the long-winded link tool is now called Search.Twitter.com.
>
> http://Search.Twitter.com is where you can search for your username or your company name and see what's being said to you or about you on Twitter.
>
> You'll still hear some people call this search tool "Summize" for a number of reasons – for one, it's much shorter.
>
> If you use http://Twummize.com it'll bring you to a site that'll give you a side by side look of your twitter stream on the left, and the search tool on your right. Very cool. If you haven't used it yet, go check it out now.

What the Heck is Twitter?

Here's what you see when you go to Search.Twitter.com:

See what the world is doing — *right now.*

Advanced Search

Search

Trending topics: Olympics, Michael Phelps, #echo, iPhone, Olympic, Georgia, T-Mobile, McCain, Clone Wars, Bigfoot

Twitter has acquired Summize! Read about it...

Twitter Home · About Twitter Search · API · Apps · Install Search Plugin

© 2008 Twitter, Inc.

You see the search box, and all the trending topics the majority of tweeters are tweeting about right now. (Another useful strategy to use.)

Simply enter the search term you want to track in the white box. In this case it is "CoachDeb" since we want to see all the people who replied to @CoachDeb to answer her question, "What is Twitter?"

Next screen that pops up will show you all the people who are talking TO you or ABOUT you.

NOTE: Keep in mind, just like with blogging, you'll see the original tweet (in this case in the form of a question) at the bottom, and the most CURRENT Tweet on top. So if you want to "follow the conversation" you'll want to read from bottom to top to read them in order.)

What is Twitter? The Twitterverse responds:

twitter | coachdeb | Search

Realtime results for coachdeb   0.23 seconds

139 more results since you started searching. Refresh to see them.

GrantGriffiths: **@CoachDeb** twitter is a community where you can interact with and learn from those you have conversations with.
10 minutes ago · Reply · View Tweet

virtuallyready: **@CoachDeb** - Love that party quote... that's great!
11 minutes ago · Reply · View Tweet · Show Conversation

andyheadworth: **@CoachDeb** Twitter is pervasive and invasive, at the same time as being an addictive and totally enjoyable way to communicate with others.
11 minutes ago · Reply · View Tweet

virtuallyready: **@CoachDeb** Twitter blends social connectivity with business allowing users to learn, expand and share knowledge quickly & efficiently
14 minutes ago · Reply · View Tweet · Show Conversation

lisamariemary: Retweeting **@CoachDeb**: "Twitter is like having a party in your pocket!" [This is so perfect - I love it! -Lisa]
15 minutes ago · Reply · View Tweet

jodonahue: **@CoachDeb** I like that picture you just painted!
16 minutes ago · Reply · View Tweet

CoachDeb: "Twitter is like having a party in your pocket!"
17 minutes ago · Reply · View Tweet

nickrice @CoachDeb how's this: twitter is a online tool that lets you send messages & talk to whomever you "follow" and whomever is following you 24 minutes ago from web in reply to CoachDeb

LisaVanAllen: **@CoachDeb** Twitter is the best and easiest social marketing tool on the web - fast updates, low maintenance, potentially high impact and fun!
16 minutes ago · Reply · View Tweet

What the Heck is Twitter?

freeace: **@CoachDeb** A short-burst communication tool.
less than a minute ago · Reply · View Tweet

alexashrugged: **@CoachDeb** It's like a ginormous chatroom/message board
1 minute ago · Reply · View Tweet

joltheartist: **@coachDeb** Twitter is like the love-child of blogging and haiku.
2 minutes ago · Reply · View Tweet

camper1: **@CoachDeb** glimpses of our meanderings through the Universe, exposed to our followers, shared for eternity! That B Twitter.
3 minutes ago · Reply · View Tweet

fredkzk: **@CoachDeb** it's a community of public instant messaging
3 minutes ago · Reply · View Tweet · ⤷ Show Conversation

TanyaW: **@CoachDeb** my virtual water cooler for social networking
less than a minute ago · Reply · View Tweet

RyanAllaire: **@coachdeb** Twitter is a tool used to inform, 'keep up with', and network like crazy..o ya- & happens to make me cash! ;-) use that as a quote
less than a minute ago · Reply · View Tweet

SharonMcP: **@CoachDeb** The online equivalent of Forbes, Business Week, Better Homes and Gardens, High Times and National Enquirer rolled into one.
2 minutes ago · Reply · View Tweet · ⤷ Show Conversation

CharlesHeflin: **@CoachDeb** Twitter is effective to get past the gatekeeper and communicate directly with top industry minds to build profitable relationships
3 minutes ago · Reply · View Tweet · ⤷ Show Conversation

smithereensblog: **@CoachDeb** Twitter is one part microblog, one part mini-forum, one part instant messaging platform, and one part crack cocaine.
4 minutes ago · Reply · View Tweet

kiwichamp: **@CoachDeb** To the point social & business communication = for alerts, tips and sharing of information and life's ups and downs
5 minutes ago · Reply · View Tweet

KevinEikenberry: **@CoachDeb** twitter is a novel way to communicate, connect, build community and learn from others
6 minutes ago · Reply · View Tweet

CoachDeb: POLL 4 Twitter Handbook: "What is Twitter?" (@ me how YOU describe Twitter in 140 or less)
9 minutes ago · Reply · View Tweet

What is Twitter? The Twitterverse responds:

Realtime results for coachdeb 0.03 seconds

 bbspress: **@CoachDeb** Twitter is like a living Rolodex that responds to you.
10 minutes ago · Reply · View Tweet · ⤶ Show Conversation

 GinaBell: **@CoachDeb** Oooh! I love Tsufit's book. A blast to read - she has a fab sense of humor.
10 minutes ago · Reply · View Tweet

 katalink : **@CoachDeb** Network weaving accelerator. Efficient multi-user multi-point micro-blogging platform. Get-job-done-with-help-from-your-friends.
12 minutes ago · Reply · View Tweet

haikutwaiku: **@coachDeb** Twitter is like the love-child of blogging and haiku.
13 minutes ago · Reply · View Tweet · ⤶ Show Conversation

Now here is what it looks in the **REPLIES** tab on Coach Deb's Twitter profile page:

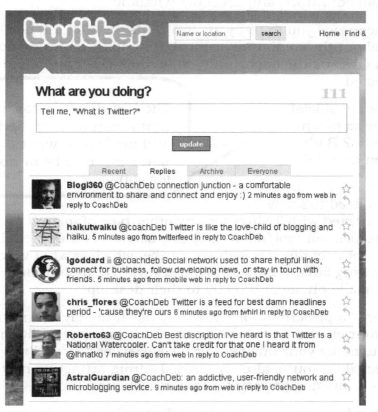

You can check out additional answers from the Tweeples of the Twitterverse to the question, *"What is Twitter"* and add YOUR answer/perspective to this question, when you visit the Twitter Revolution online at this specific post:

http://twitterhandbook.com/blog/what-is-twitter

Every time this question is asked in the Twitterverse, and people post their comments here, we learn a few more ways that people are using Twitter. This is the magic and beauty of Twitter, and why we've become Twitter addicts.

For your amusement, here's a funny TwitAholic video you may either relate to or laugh at. Either way you'll be highly entertained: http://snipurl.com/twitaddict

We encourage you to put your two cents in. After all, new media is all about the community contributing to the conversation, which gives us the opportunity to become wiser and more connected.

What's my official answer as to what Twitter is? Both Warren and Deb agree:

The beauty of Twitter is that it can be morphed and made into what *you* want it to be or do for you.

All you need to know to get started with Twitter (or any other type of instant communication tool/micro-blogging service) is that it enables you to connect directly with your tribe, which is what we call your raving fans, clients or members, via an instant message to their mobile phone or directly to their desktop.

Twitter is a powerful tool if you only use it to stay connected with your clients. But it can be used a number of additional ways to make your business or life easier, better, and more connected as you've already noticed – from attracting new clients to making powerful, new connections.

Deborah has several accounts on Twitter and she explains how she uses and manages each one:

@**CoachDeb** is what we refer to as "Chatty Debi." She's the chatty one that gets involved, has multiple conversations at once, connects with tweeple, talks about topics, brings up polls, and asks lots of questions to get her tribe communicating and debating with one another.

@**DeborahMicek** is my professional account name. She's very quiet. I use this profile much less frequently than my @**CoachDeb** profile. Since many people have looked up my full name from the 1st book I wrote and added me on that account (despite very little activity), I started using it to share industry resources, breaking news, apps, and links for my friends to know about.

Many of my friends in the internet marketing world follow me on my quiet @**DeborahMicek** profile and have phone notifications turned ON because they know they're not going to see more than a few tweets a month, and never more than a few in one day.

One of my VAs runs the @**BLOGi360** account. This is the "product/software" profile where we track and manage our reputation online for the blogging platform we created, and answer our member's questions or remind them of upcoming Webinars for them to join that day—just in case they missed an email or are on the road.

Additionally, I have a few other accounts that are private and not publicized, as they are only shared with my coaching clients. These accounts are marked private and users need to request to follow me on these profiles. This is how you can keep certain information and communication private and shared ONLY with your tribe, clients, friends or families, knowing others aren't lurking into your stream.

Warren Whitlock also uses two accounts. Deborah follows him on both, and vice versa.

@**WarrenWhitlock** is his active account that he tweets from daily. His other account @**BookWarren** was one of his original accounts he used, which branded both his name and what he's known for—making authors rich.

You can have several different accounts and use Twitter for a variety of different reasons. It enables quick and instant communication with your prospects and clients waiting to become your tribe, friend, and connection.

When anyone asks, "What is Twitter?" my mind starts going in all different directions because it really is different things to different people. It's simply not a thing you can neatly fit in a box, because quite frankly, Twitter has become something very different from what it was when it was first created.

When I sat down and started really thinking about what Twitter is and what it could be used for so we could explain it here in this book for you, I came up with a top ten list that we'll be revealing to you throughout this book.

You'll also learn a lot of tips to increase your influence on Twitter. It's not just a book about the nuts and bolts about Twitter. It's a guide for you to increase your connections, influence and impact using a very simple tool.

The more you keep your mind open to new ideas from the stories we share, the more you'll open yourself up to that innovative idea in your industry that no one else is doing yet!

And THAT is the true secret to the power of Twitter.

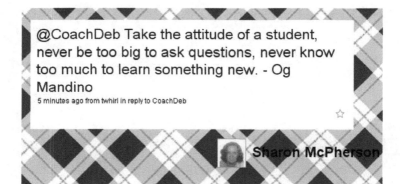

@CoachDeb Take the attitude of a student, never be too big to ask questions, never know too much to learn something new. - Og Mandino

5 minutes ago from twhirl in reply to CoachDeb

Sharon McPherson

Chapter 3

How to Get Started With Twitter

Twitter began as an easy way to keep people posted on what you are up to at this very moment. What are you doing?

This has continued to be the spirit of Twitter and quite frankly, it's what gives it its seductive appeal. (We'll elaborate more on the seduction of Twitter in a later chapter.)

But it's grown and morphed into something drastically different as its users have defined how they enjoy using the service.

Lee LeFever from Common Craft (CommonCraft.com/show) created one of the best early videos describing the power of how Twitter works.

You can watch this video on the TwitterHandbook.com blog and tell us what you think by placing a comment so other readers will see your thoughts.

Here's the short url that you can fit in a tweet to share with others getting started with twitter:

http://snipurl.com/CommonCraft

Here is the number one question to ask yourself when crafting your Twitter strategy.

*How can I get my message across to my friends, clients, fans, subscribers and future customers in a **value-added** way?*

Twitter is simply the micro-blogging tool that allows you to connect with your clients directly on their cell phone or computer in a non-obtrusive way.

(Note: As of this writing, watching the "Trending Topics" on Search.Twitter.com, I learned that Twitter stopped the ability of send and receive messages to mobile phones outside the United States of America due to the costs involved. Hopefully, they'll figure out a monetization model where people can pay for this service in order to get it back in their respective countries by the time this book gets around the world.

If Twitter does not address this issue and discover a way to bring that feature back into their service, I'm confident another service will rise up on the internet to take Twitter's place.

Perhaps by the time this book comes off the printing press, we'll have already announced this new service that we're helping our clients navigate through in the ONLINE version of this book @ http://TwitterHandbook.com

From my discussions with several programmers on Twitter, an open source API is currently in development.

So keep in mind, wherever we say "Twitter" in this book, you can easily replace it with whatever "micro-blogging service" you choose to use—especially when the next best thing comes in to compete and take its place and is the NEXT hottest place for people to congregate online.)

The nicest thing about being able to contact people through Twitter (or any micro-blogging service that allows you to send text messages to mobile phones) is that customers don't have to give you their cell phone numbers which they're apprehensive to share with any company. Rather, Twitter allows them to follow you on Twitter in order to get your updates, alerts, tips, etc. and keep the power in their hands.

The moment you start sending spammy tweets that annoy your followers with too many blatant ads that are uninteresting or unwanted, they've got the power to simply "unfollow you" or turn mobile notifications OFF for your account name.

So the key tip here is **make an impact with every tweet you make.**

It really all boils down to how much of an influence you make and how persuasive your tweets are. But we'll cover that topic in a later chapter.

For now, let's get you started on the right path and shorten your learning curve so you get the best results when using Twitter or any other online social network of choice.

The point of this book is not to repeat resources that are currently out there, but to direct you to them, and then offer a unique approach to using Twitter for business, brand building, etc. Getting started with the basics of Twitter can be followed best by starting with the site itself: http://Twitter.com

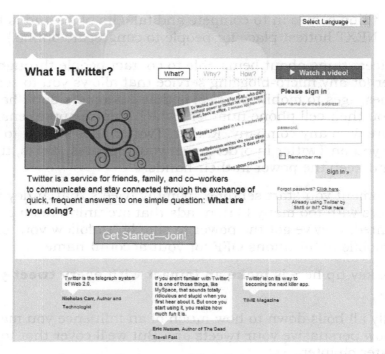

Hit the green button that says, "Get Started—Join!" Then sign up! It's as easy as that!

But there are a few things to consider when signing up, starting with selecting the right username.

This next tip will save you the trouble of having to change your username later.

Create a Free Twitter Account

Username:	CoachDeb	Your URL: http://twitter.com/**CoachDeb**
	Username can only contain letters, numbers and '_'	
Password:		6 characters or more (be tricky!)
Email Address:		In case you forget something
Humanness:		

bench KA

Type the two words:

reCAPTCHA™
stop spam.
read books.

☐ I want the inside scoop—please send me email updates!

By clicking on 'I accept' below, you confirm that you are over 13 years of age and accept the **Terms of Service**.

I accept. Create my account.

© 2008 Twitter About Us Contact Blog Status Downloads API Help Jobs TOS Privacy

There are a few things to point out in the username that are important to pay attention to. Note how Deb differentiates her brand "Coach" from her name "Deb" by using capital letters. Note how there is NO _ underscore _ or numbers in her username, making it easy to tweet from an iPhone or other mobile phone without having to shift to another screen every time your friends send you an @ message.

INSIDER TIP: Underscores in a name indicate you're not one of the early birds who joined Twitter and there's no reason to call attention to that. Plus, if someone already has your name locked up, you do NOT want to just put an _ underscore _ in your username to differentiate it, because you'll inadvertently drive traffic and visitors to the other person's page to follow him/her instead of YOU. (Not good.)

It's perfectly acceptable to use your full name, and I'd advise you to lock up your full name (first and last name) if it's available. (That way no one else can brand jack your name.) Just don't add your middle initial or make your name any longer than it needs to be.

Challenges with using your full name arise when it's long and/or difficult for new friends/followers to remember the spelling. If that's the case, you may want to consider using your BRAND as your username instead. Like what Scott did.

Here's how @ScottTousignant changed his long French username to his brand that he's now famous for. *(Ok, admittedly after much insisting on my part. But this is where I get away with "nagging" with my brand, by calling it "coaching." Fortunately, Scott is much appreciative. Right, Scott?)* Now, Scott is known as @TheFitB on Twitter, and has hundreds of followers who send him messages very easily.

IMPORTANT TIP: Scott still KEPT his full name parked and simply left his last tweet notifying anyone who finds him there where they can go and follow him actively.

There are several advantages of using a short brand name, versus your full name. Naturally this decision will be determined by your own social networking strategy.

Some business professionals want to brand their name, so they'll use their full name on Twitter. But if you're looking to let people know what you do through your username, incorporating your brand into your username is a quick start way to do that.

Benefits of using a brand name vs. your full name:

For starters, it's easy to remember, spell, and type when using a mobile device to communicate with you. Now when people are tweeting @TheFitB, they have more room to share their thoughts because his name isn't that long, hogging all the characters in the tweet.

But the best secret of this "short branded username" that you'll create for yourself is that you'll be branding yourself on ALL social networks! You'll have a unique brand that will **differentiate** you from all the other tweeters who are simply using their names.

TIP: The key is to <u>be remembered.</u>

My UNIQUE branded username uniquely available on ALL social networks is:

@_____

Deborah reveals her secret as to why she prefers to tweet using her brand @CoachDeb instead of her full name @DeborahMicek

*"Every tweet you make becomes **its own Web page.** When clients are doing a Google search for my name, "Deborah Micek" I'd prefer they see all the published articles I've written for Entrepreneur Magazine, the Honolulu Star Bulletin, links to our book "Secrets to Online Persuasion", or articles on my blog, TribalSeduction.com rather than a bunch of inane @ tweets that mean nothing when standing on its own."*

Note: This is most tweeples "Ah-HA moment."

Go ahead... give it to yourself. You know you want to. Ahhhhhh!

Another challenge when trying to reserve your full name may come into play with Twitter's love-affair with placing "limits" on everything.

Twitter limits your username to 14 characters or less. So as long as your name is not too long for Twitter's limitations on usernames, like Armando Montelongo's name is, then take it.

If not, you can do what Armando did and grab your last name (@Montelongo). He also grabbed his brand from his TV show on A&E, @FlipThisHouse, where he tweets about behind the scenes activities for his fans to follow the show there.

Ahhhh Crapolla! Now I'm stuck with a bad username!?!

(Note Crapolla is an old Italian word from the old country. In case you were unfamiliar with that technical term meaning, oh-my-goodness-now-what-am-I-gonna-do?)

If you're reading this right now getting all ticked off that you didn't have this information months ago when you reserved your username and you feel you're now stuck with a long_username_with_an_underscore in it—fear not! It's very easy to change your username on Twitter. This is where they are very different than services like Facebook or MySpace that lock you into a username the moment you choose it.

Below are the steps to changing your username if you are frustrated with the one you have now.

How to Change Your Username on Twitter And Keep All Your Followers

You simply change your current username to your new username in the settings section on Twitter. Then quickly reserve your old username under a different email address so you won't lose any links from all your previous tweets.

Everything else as far as your followers/following remains the same – well – except your username/TwitID ☺ LOL

Sharon McPherson wanted to start using a shorter username so her friends would have more room when tweeting her.

Let's use her username as an example for you to see how simple it is to change your name and have all the same followers.

Example:

1. Change SharonMcPherson to Sharon McP under Settings/Account in the Username area of your current account.

2. Lock up your old username (SharonMcPherson) by creating a new Twitter account under a different email address (this is where gmail.com comes in handy).

3. Tweet your followers so they recognize your new username in their Twitter stream as "the new you" – they don't have to do anything, all your followers remain the same, they'll just see a new name when you pop up.

Turn on your mobile phone

Simply go to Settings/Devices in your Twitter account and enter your mobile phone number. Once you do this, and hit SAVE, you'll see a green password that will come up.

You'll immediately receive a text message on your mobile phone, and you'll need to reply back to that number with the password given to you in this section.

Save that number in your contacts as "Twitter" so you can easily tweet from your phone.

WARNING: Be sure to check with your mobile phone provider before turning on mobile notifications to see what the fees are for sending and receiving text messages. I recommend you get the unlimited plan and start following at least 10 of your friends and 10 influential tweeters on your phone so you can get the feel for what people are tweeting and how it feels to receive messages using your mobile phone.

The moment it gets too much, simply send the word "off" to Twitter on your mobile phone, and you will not receive any tweets until you send "on" to Twitter. Otherwise, you'll just receive direct messages, or whatever you decide when you're in the Settings/Device tab on Twitter.

Now you can track keywords, your username, and all sorts of things you want to follow on your mobile phone simply by sending the word Track and whatever keyword you want to follow.

For example, I track Hawaii on my phone, simply by sending this text message to Twitter:

```
Track Hawaii
```

Anytime I want to untrack Hawaii, I can either tweet track Hawaii again, or send:

Untrack Hawaii

and I immediately receive confirmation that I will no longer receive notifications with Hawaii in them.

For more tips on using your mobile phone with Twitter, get updated codes and strategies in the online Twitter Handbook at:

TwitterHandbook.com/blog/mobile

There is something about feeling connected with others that make us feel a part of each other's lives. It's this basic tribal nature of who we are as human beings.

The moment you begin using your mobile phone to track your keywords, name, and top 10-25 influential tweeters who you follow, you'll begin the addictive journey that we call Tweeting. Enjoy the journey! Welcome to the Twitterverse!

Oh! Before we forget! Be sure to follow us and send us each an @ msg once you join in so we can help keep you informed on all the things that change lightning fast in the Twitterverse that you need to know of.

http://Twitter.com/CoachDeb
http://Twitter.com/WarrenWhitlock

You can also add us and follow our alternate accounts:

http://Twitter.com/DeborahMicek
http://Twitter.com/BookWarren

Chapter 4

Ten Steps to Attract a Flood of Followers

Fast Track Your Success on Twitter
with these top 10 tips

Tip 1: If you're not on Twitter, join right away with a unique username.

Lock up your name, and use a short and unique name as your username. Avoid using a middle name on Twitter. You only have 140 characters available. Your name uses some of that valuable space. If you're reserving your full name, use your first and last name ONLY. A middle initial will just confuse people. You'll wind up driving traffic to somebody else's username without the middle initial. If someone already has your name, be creative. Use something else, something unique.

Avoid using numbers or underscores in your username. Spammers are forced to use numbers, so when veteran users of Twitter see someone following them with numbers in their usernames, they're likely to not only not follow you, but block you from following them.

Currently, there is no copy and paste on the iPhone, a popular mobile phone Tweeters use. You'll force followers to go through three steps just to tweet your name using an underscore. It's aggravating, and it will limit replies to you when they are mobile Tweeting.

One option in getting a unique username is to blend your brand with your name. We discussed this in an earlier chapter in detail. This one tip can really help you get more followers not just here on Twitter but on all the social networks that are created just like Twitter. If your name is short and unique, people will be able to find you on every other social network that's created.

Follow the example of Robert Scoble who started blogging when he worked for Microsoft as himself, NOT Microsoft. Now that he's not with them any longer, his BRAND is still in tact, "The Scobleizer" (AKA: @Scobleizer on Twitter). Follow him. And follow his lead. He's the master at starting great conversations. I modeled much of my tweeting habits after his style of communication.

Get his book while you're at it, "Naked Conversations" by Robert Scoble. Everything in his book about blogging can be directly applied to Twitter, a micro-blogging platform.

TIP: You still need to lock up your company's name on any social network out there. You can use that profile for more company specific alerts, announcements, news or tips. We recommend you grab your brand or company name and lock all these up under different email accounts. Even if you don't actively use these accounts, you need to have them so no one brandjacks your company username. (More on brand-jacking in a later chapter.)

You heard it here first:

Twitter usernames will become valuable real estate just like Web sites were back in the 90's. So – lock 'em up!

Tip 2: When you join first join Twitter, put a picture up immediately—before following anyone.

A visual picture of who you are is the first thing Tweeters will look at when deciding whether to follow you or not.

When you start following people, they'll come to your site to check you out and determine if you're follow-worthy. They first want to make sure you're a "real person" and not just some spammy Twitter-bot auto-following everyone under the sun.

If you're a small business owner, sales professional, realtor, marketer, or any other type of business executive, be sure to use a recent picture of yourself so when you attend in-person conferences, you'll be immediately recognized.

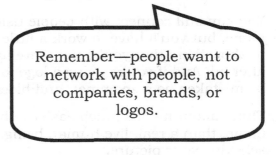

Remember—people want to network with people, not companies, brands, or logos.

There is a debate over whether to use a real picture versus an avatar. With very few exceptions given to some of the early adopters who used avatars "to be different" like @DaveTaylor, I advise my clients to use real pictures if they're interested in making real connections. But it's an individual decision based on what social media strategy you've got in place. Some tweeters wish to disguise their identity so they prefer a cartoon or avatar instead of a real picture.

Dave Taylor gets away with it, because he's already well-known in the "Blog World Community" and was on Twitter in the very beginning. But recently, there was a big hoop-la over a new tool where people could create avatars (aka: cartoons) of themselves. While this may be fun to do for a day or two, it's not a long-term, wise business strategy unless you're not interested in making an influential impact.

Using an avatar or logo puts a barrier up between your face and your followers. Using your own picture allows for greater intimacy and connection. So if you're looking to attract tons of followers, try using your picture compared to an avatar and see the difference it makes.

You may lock up your company name and brand on Twitter as we've recommended in previous chapters. Just keep in mind for your active Twitter profile, that if you're using your company name to get to know people, it's more formal and impersonal, therefore, people will put up instant barriers when they see you tweet.

You can still connect with people using a brand, or company name, but you'll have to work a little harder to gain their trust, to show them that you're not there just to spam them with ad after ad. And if you're using a logo for your picture, you could be mistaken as a spammer, and blocked inadvertently.

Think about it – it's much easier to block a faceless brand name, than a real, live human being. Keep that in mind when selecting your picture.

Exception to this rule is the corporations using Twitter to serve as a resource for their customers – like @comcastcares. That's when you want your brand logo in there. We do this with @SaleZy our Blog i360 character on Twitter, but it's a private account for client communication only, versus an account to win new clients and build new relationships. See the difference?

Tip 3: Tweet a few things that leave a lasting impact before you start following people or looking for followers.

Have at least 5-8 tweets up on your profile to give new visitors coming across your page an idea of what type of tweets they can expect if they choose to follow you.

Be an influencer. Be a tweeter who adds value. Offer tips, resources, links to valuable sites (NOT just your own— especially when you first start out.)

We recommend the last tweet you update before you start following people, is in the form of a question. Remember, it's the questions that drive us. And it's an exceptional human being who can resist answering a well thought-out question.

> But don't just take my word for it. What do you think? Do you think questions stir up other thoughts in the minds of your readers?

Don't just tweet, "I have an update," and then not have a picture on your site, and not have any tweets for them to see either. You will not get a flood of followers adding you without a picture, and having at least a few tweets up unless they're on auto-follow.

What can you Tweet when you first get started?

You could tweet a few cool things about yourself, perhaps industry tips, quotes, questions, anything you'd put in your "About You" page on a traditional Web site. You then can start following and connecting with people.

Don't just talk about your business at first either. (Snore!)

Instead, talk about WHO you ARE. Unless of course, you have no personality and are as interesting as a fig on a tree. If that's the case, and the only thing you ever talk about with any of your friends when you get together at a party is work, then perhaps Twitter is not the right place for you to attract your ideal audience for your business.

Remember, many people come on Twitter to get a break from work. If you're just talking about paperwork, you'll not only come across as a boring individual, you won't attract a flood of followers either. Be interesting.

Link to your bio online, or your blog so people can get more information about you, your writing style, your skill sets when you first start tweeting.

People understand that you're just getting started. That's okay. Provide a few tweets and then start following people of interest to you. Just remember, with every tweet you make, be follow-worthy.

Tip 4: Hook up an application to help you track and monitor the tweets coming at you.

You have several options to choose from, which goes to show you the trend Twitter has started with the overwhelming number of apps available to support Twitter no matter what type of browser, computer or mobile phone you prefer to use while tweeting.

Twhirl http://twhirl.org is good for people who are on a PC or a MAC. One of the great things about using Twhirl is that it connects to multiple micro-blogging sites including Twitter, identi.ca, Friendfeed and seesmic accounts. There are a lot more things twhirl can do to improve your twitter experience, and it offers various configuration options to adapt to your personal needs.

Twitterific is for Mac users only, but works very much like Twhirl.

TwitterFox is a Firefox extension that notifies you of your friends' tweets of Twitter. (Previously known as TwitterNotifier) This extension adds a tiny icon on the status bar that notifies you when your friends update their tweets. Also it has a small text input field to update your tweets.

http://www.naan.net/trac/wiki/TwitterFox

TweetDeck http://TweetDeck.com has become a favorite of many tweeters at the time of this writing. TweetDeck enables users to split their main feed (All Tweets) into topic or group specific columns allowing a broader overview of tweets. To do this All Tweets are saved to a local database. The far left column will always contain All Tweets. The GROUP, SEARCH and REPLIES buttons then allow the user to make up additional columns populated from the database. Once created these additional columns will automatically update allowing the user to keep track of a twitter threads far easier.

There are other cool apps you can use to enhance your Twitter experience, but we'll include that in the APPS chapter (and

continue updating in the online version of this book at:
http://TwitterHandbook.com/blog/apps

These are just to get you started.

Tip 5: Turn on your mobile phone and track influential tweeters to engage them when they tweet.

Go into the settings in the phone and make sure it's turned on. Set it to nudge you daily to remind you to tweet at least once a day.

Set up your mobile phone to get all the direct messages to you. I've heard people say, "It would wake me up in the middle of the night." There is a setting where you can easily turn off notifications when you go to bed. You can have it set to turn off at 11:00 p.m., and come back on around 7:00 a.m.

Personally, I'll admit it, "My name is @CoachDeb and I'm a TwitAholic."

I've never been a morning person, but I no longer need an alarm clock to wake me up early for tennis any longer. People start tweeting me before my alarm ever goes off. What wakes me up is the sun shining on my face, the real birds outside chirping, and the tweeting birds that come from my tweeting friends from my iPhone resting on my night stand. I know why I'm addicted to Twitter. And if you use Twitter properly, you'll soon join the Tribe of TwitAholics.

Using Twitter on your phone will help you stay connected in a way that isn't possible on other types of social networks like MySpace or Facebook.

Part of the seduction of Twitter is the instant connections it gives you by being able to connect with people from anywhere to anywhere—all from your mobile phone.

A popular twitter app for the iPhone is **Twinkle**
http://tapulous.com/twinkle It allows you to Tweet easily from
your iPhone. Very cool app.

You can also simply use the mobile version of Twitter by going
to http://m.twitter.com/home using your browser on your cell
phone.

Hahlo is a nice desktop application for your iPhone or iTouch.
It's an application to monitor and track your Twitter activity.

**Tip 6: Bookmark www.Twummize.com on your desktop and
your mobile phone.**

Twummize is simply the short cut link used to get directly to
search.twitter and cleverly use it side by side in your browser.

The long URL for this search tool is http://search.twitter.com.

Once you go to www.Twummize.com put in your user name. Let
that come up and save it as a bookmark on your desktop and to
your home page of your iPhone.

Track your username, company name and full name daily in
order to respond to the people who are sending you messages
whether they use the @ symbol in front of their tweet, or in the
middle of their tweet. This way, you'll know when people are
talking to you, with you, or about you.

MEGA TIP:
Once you get used to tracking your own username, you'll also
want to add your top favorite Tweeters to your iPhone or your
bookmarks on your desktop to visit them daily, see what they're
up to and get involved in the conversation.

I like using Twummize.com for the split screen it creates for you
automatically when using Search.Twitter.com. Plus, when
talking about it on Twitter, it's a much shorter way of referring
to this search tool, especially when we're all on a limit of 140
characters with every tweet we make.

Tip 7: Make sure you use the replies tab.

Newbies, don't feel bad! I can't tell you how many gurus in internet marketing have tweeted, "I just found the replies tab!" People have been talking to them all this time since they first joined, wondering why they were being "ignored."

Don't be "that guy." Use your replies tab and use it often.

When you see your Twitter stream at www.Twitter.com/home, there is a "recent" tab which you see automatically. To the right of that is the "replies" tab.

When you click on your "replies tab", you'll be able to see all the people talking to you. (Or as we say in the Twitterverse, talking @ you.) Try not to ignore them unless you're getting too many replies. In that case, select the ones that contribute the most value to your followers so they'll be able to expand their knowledge.

NOTE: If you reply to every single @ reply sent to you, (which is what I used to do) you may be accused of being "too noisy" (a tech term that means some geeks just can't keep up with your conversation). You can be selective. Look at all of them, but you don't have to always reply to all of them.

Remember, Twitter is all about PR, brand recognition and reputation management. When you get your face in front of the influencers you want to connect with and continue to offer valuable resources, you'll quickly experience the benefits of using a service like Twitter.

Tip 8: Use DM to connect with people and track trending topics

Once you begin to have a conversation sending @ messages to one particular tweeter, take it "offline" and send DM's instead. (DM = direct messages in your Twitter profile.) One of the powerful ways to use Twitter is to initiate the conversation but allow the deeper connection to take place using another communication channel, either IM, Skype chat, Gtalk, FriendFeed, Ustream or even the old fashioned communication tool sitting on your desk called the telephone.

Find out what people are talking about. Get engaged in the conversation. That's how you'll attract a larger following.

There are a few tools that track the conversations for you that you can use cleverly in order to attract more followers who are just like you!

www.Twitturly.com tracks the URLs people are talking about live. You can see the different URLs or blog links they're talking about. It gives you the ability to be first to comment.

It could be people you don't know yet. Don't just talk to people you know or your own tribe of people who are fans and clients. Think about connecting to the broader Twitterverse. I promise you'll get smarter.

http://www.twitscoop.com/

Through an automated algorithm, twitscoop crawls hundreds of tweets every minute and extracts the words which are mentioned more often than usual. The result is displayed in a Tag Cloud, using the following rule: **the hotter, the bigger** (no joke here).

http://Search.Twitter.com shows you the top 10 trending topics to allow you to find out what's going on in the world, and participate in the conversations happening in the Twitterverse.

Tip 9: Increase Your Influence Rank on Twitter by having conversations:

Getting @ replies is something that's tracked to measure your level of influence on a social network like Twitter. The more @'s you have, the higher you'll rise in the stats measurement of influential tweeters using conversation analytics.

Currently, Twitter Analytics are daily tracked on TwitStat, visible to all Tweeters. http://twitstat.com

Twitstat - Real time Twitter Analytics

Want to be in this list? Just follow @twitstat.

As I was writing this chapter, someone sent me the following tweet based on my rank on Twitter Analytics.

danlopez2012: **@CoachDeb** Wow grrl, your listed as having perfect tweets!?!? No wonder you wrote the book!!
about 5 hours ago · Reply · View Tweet

Perfect tweets, past 14 days	
539	prp2
235	nwjerseyliz
207	jinon
170	brampitoyo
170	NAzTListening
165	aqfery
160	petersantilli
142	CoachDeb
116	eduo
107	nichelady

There are many different things to get ranked on, so this is one goal you can set for yourself, to get on one of these lists since Tweeters often go here to find cool people to follow.

There is a Top 10 list, a Most Engaging list (measuring how many conversations you're having) and most replies to list:

Most replies to, past 14 days	
392	erwblo
328	marketingfacts
293	rotjong
260	coachdeb
259	puur
251	isheila
244	vangeest
241	frankmeeuwsen
232	marlooz
224	having

There's even a most social, most happy and most angry list. So no matter what you're personality – you can easily get on one of these lists – if you set it as a goal for yourself.

The biggest secret to attracting more followers – is to have conversations! Be engaging and be a leader in starting conversations. Ask stimulating questions. Most of all, remember that listening is the other part of having conversations. If you're only following 14 people and wonder why more people aren't following you, now you know the reason.

Oh, and the more entertaining you can be, the more your followers will think of you fondly when you show up in their Twitter stream, and therefore pay attention to you.

The day I got on the "funny people" list, I printed out a screen shot, placed it on my partner's desk and proclaimed, "SEE – I'm funny! Now there's PROOF!" ☺

Funny people, past 14 days	
58	erwblo
56	marketingfacts
50	coachdeb
45	rotjong
40	isheila
40	puur
39	jojanneke
39	markies
37	msh2006
36	frankmeeuwsen

Tip 10: Sign up for www.TwitPic.com

When accessing your TwitPic account in order to begin uploading pictures, your username is the same as Twitter. You are already a member there automatically as a result of having a Twitter profile. Now all you need to do is start uploading pictures!

BONUS TIPS TO ATTRACT A FLOOD OF FOLLOWERS

> It may take you a month or so after you set up a Twitter profile and get used to it before you move to these bonus tips, and that's ok. Move to this next phase at your own pace.
>
> But we had to include them in this book, because this is where you'll begin to see a boost in your followers and clients as a result of taking Twitter to the next level.

BONUS Tip 11: Sign up for www.Jott.com so you can talk & tweet!

When you send a voice message to Jott, it comes through as a Tweet when you give it that command. You'll not only see the messages coming in from Jott, transcribed for you as a tweet, but you can click on the link and hear the voice message that was left for Jott. Voice is a powerful way to connect with people. So is video.

BONUS Tip 12: Sign up for 12seconds.TV

http://12seconds.tv

This gives you the ability to send short video messages (yep! You guessed it! 12 seconds long) so that your followers can SEE you and connect with you on an even deeper level.

BONUS Tip 13: The next step in using video is going LIVE streaming using http://www.Ustream.TV or Mogulus.com.

Tell people you are going live. Chat about whatever your industry topic is. And let your face and voice be known on a deeper level.

Are you starting to see why I'm so against the use of Avatars as your primary profile image?

You want to gradually allow your followers to get to know you. Your face. Your voice. Your face and voice is where they get to see eye contact and body language which helps them feel more and more comfortable with you (provided you're a nice, likeable person) which all helps to build trust, earn credibility, and become an established authority in your industry or niche in the minds of your future clients. This attracts people to not only follow you on Twitter, but to do business with you again and again as a result of meeting you on Twitter.

See how the connections all lead to making money using Twitter, but not "directly" or "overtly"?

You can segue to make those connections into product sales. It's simple. You don't tweet through a conversion process. Rather you take the conversation OFF Twitter and bring it into your webinar or TV room, that you set up whatever number of channels in your Ustream room. You can THEN convert those you've attracted who need your product or service in these alternate settings. It could be a simple phone call. You know, that old fashioned machine that sits in the corner of your desk collecting dust. Yeah, that one. It's okay to pick it up and use it once in a while.

You can see Coach Deb's various channels on Ustream via: http://www.ustream.tv/CoachDeb or http://www.ustream.tv/channel/idebi.tv.

You can model the set up, but make it fit your personality style. The key is being authentically you. But this is how you get the sales or do your sales pitch and drive them to your site where they can easily invest in your products or services.

Just remember: Get permission first and be conversational and then people will ask YOU where they can buy from you. That's the secret.

BONUS Tip 14: Copy and paste your Twitter badge code and use it on your blogs, Websites, and Blog i360 hub sites.

You'll see this right beside your profile on your Twitter home page.

You'll see a badge link. When you first set up your Twitter profile, there is a link. It says something like, "Put your badge on your other sites." You can also just go directly to: http://twitter.com/badges when you're logged in to Twitter, and select what type, color, shape, size of your badge and it'll automatically create a code for you based on what social networking profile you want to use it on. It's that simple!

Copy the code and put it on your BLOG i360 system, Facebook profile or MySpace in the "about me" section. Every time you tweet, you're also updating your Facebook, Friend Feed, blog and MySpace at the same time. Pretty cool, eh?

BONUS Tip 15: Set up Friend Feed http://FriendFeed.com.

Friend Feed is another one of our favorite new social networks. It's not an application. It's an alternative to take conversations off Twitter over to Friend Feed. It does a great job of tracking the actual conversation you're having about a particular subject. You can also see how much your followers like a particular resource you share because they can favorite it by giving it a "thumbs up" check indicating they like it.

http://FriendFeed.com/CoachDeb
http://FriendFeed.com/WarrenWhitlock

The beautiful thing about Friend Feed is you can plug in your username and pull in feeds directly from Twitter. Add your YouTube profile and Flickr username for photo sharing. Then pull in your blog feed so all your content you upload each day is found in one place.

Coach Deb has had great success with her Friend Feed "I had people adding me there constantly despite the fact that I'm not there as often as I am on Twitter. But it doesn't matter because as long as I'm tweeting, I'm feeding my Friend Feed. See how that works? You "feed" your stream all because you set up a brilliant social network using the same username you've become famous for on another social network.

@Scobleizer (Robert Scoble) was the 1st tweeter who turned me on to Friend Feed and I'm thrilled I have phone notifications turned ON for Robert, because I always get the best tech resources from him, not to mention interesting conversation starters that I can't help but jump in and share my two cents worth in reply (or as we say in Twitterland, my $1.40 worth).

When I first set up my Friend Feed account, I pulled in all the feeds from my blogs: TribalSeduction.com/blog/feed, 60secondMotivators.com/blog/feed, and a few others, so no matter what day I was posting on one of my blogs, simultaneously I will have had automatically updated my Friend Feed page too!

I added my YouTube and Flickr account, where I also go by Coach Deb. As a result, my Friend Feed was being fed every day, even though I wasn't personally there in weeks!"

Friend Feed pulls in content from all your feeds. That's the beauty of bringing all this together in one organized place.

We predict that Friend Feed is going to be a really popular place—if just for the fact that it doesn't need a lot of tender loving care on a daily basis by you manually in order to serve you well.

Chapter 5

How to Be Follow Worthy

From the beginning, we've been saying, "No Rules for being on Twitter." We still stick to this philosophy. But you should be familiar with what the Twitterverse likes and dislikes when choosing to follow tweeters – especially if you want to be follow-worthy.

We came across a great post by @LynnTerry who compiled tweets on her blog ClickNews.com to address this matter – by the people for the people.

This time you're getting tips straight from the trenches. Real answers from real people about what they like and dislike about twitter, and the people who tweet there. Thanks Lynn for putting this list together and granting permission to republish your post in Twitter Revolution!

DISCLAIMER: *All tweets left "as is" spelling errors, typos and shorthand sentences left intact to give you the flair of how tweets are written on Twitter.*

Q: What makes you follow someone on Twitter?

@casthompson: two words - <u>subject matter</u>.

@Mgkchild: Their experiences and <u>what I can learn from them</u>.

@KayBallard: Excellent question. I am fairly new to twitter. I think it takes a while to learn who to follow. For me, it will change over time

@charleslau: I follow because I want to see what in the world this person is doing, and also to update me on his web stuff...

@cassiegermsheid: Cuz they're <u>interesting, controversial, funny, smart</u> or I like the links they offer (as long as they're provided with good content)

@charlestonpchlp: if they <u>offer information</u> for having an online business, or other interesting info. big plus if they live in the area

@RoyMontero: When they point me to <u>resources</u>, resources, resources that resonate with me!

@christinalemmey: I follow <u>biz contacts</u>, well known names or <u>people who add to conversations</u>

@jonathanbentz: i follow ppl if i have an interest in what they say. if a persons blog can keep my interest and they have twitter, i follow.

@aomoon: when that person is authenticate, true to himself/herself

@Mgkchild: I agree with getting to know them. There's some with experience I'm looking for, but would not want to assoc. with.

@SharonMcP: If I see <u>active participation</u> on someone's Twitter page I'll follow, even if their biz is not related to mine. That's networking.

@StacieBennett: Usually it is because it is <u>someone I like</u> and like to hear what they have to say (you!) and to network and <u>learn new things</u>

@lindastacy: I follow people I know and trust, who offer <u>great tips</u>, to build relationships, and to <u>hear about recommended or new resources</u>.

@lynntay: I follow either if they have <u>fun/interesting</u> tweets or they have <u>informative/business</u> related posts, or I like the person in gen.

@KurtScholle: I follow the twitterati for getting to know stuff (re: your excellent work), <u>news flashes and ideas</u> that are expressed.

@lynntay: I also follow most people who follow me... unless it's obvious they don't tweet.

@lisastoops: - I follow those I think I can learn something from.

@danreinhold: Hmmm...Familiar names & those on more than one trusted account. Still getting the hang of it all.

@LynnTerry: Great responses! I'll answer too: I follow for <u>new contacts</u>, to <u>build relationships</u>, to hear news & <u>find resources</u>, or because I LIKE them.

Q: What makes you UN-follow someone on Twitter?

@jenngivler: updates every 5 seconds about every tiny thing they do... I like to get to know someone, but it CAN go too far LOL!

@SharonMcP: No active participation or if all the person tweets are links to buy= unfollow.

@lindastacy: I don't follow strangers who have no info on their profile and I stop following over-tweaters (too much about nothing)

@davenavarro: unfollow reason = never responds to messages.

@jonathanbentz: i unfollow if some1 is at an extreme - either very inactive or VERY spammy with their tweets

@Tsoniki: Unfollow if I follow for a specific reason and find they don't project that on twitter (may still read blog, visit website, etc.)

@StacieBennett: A lot of foul language! or vulgar stuff. Have 13 year old that likes to look over my shoulder some, she doesn't need to see that!

@lynntay: unfollow = annoying self inflated attitude - constant selling, self promoting, bragging.

@latarahamying: I follow when they are a fit for my business or personal Twitter and i unfollow when they are spammers or they twitter seldom

@steveinidaho: I unfollow when any one person seems to dominate my Twirl window and doesn't seem to be saying anything useful or interesing...

@mfartr: Promoting affiliate products, excessive drivel, excessive self promotion

@cassiegermsheid: I don't mind ppl posting ONE aff link but posting it multiple times makes me unfollow. Also, ppl who only post links every tweet.

@steveinidaho: idk, truthfully. I unfollowed one who seemed interesting at first, but just kept sending "fluff" tweets - "thx, John", etc.

@FaireNews: excessive use of chattalk and smilies will make me unfollow. There are a gazillion words out there, use them.

Q: How do you define Twitter Spam? What separates an update from a spam-tweet?

@zemote: spam tweets are when people follow thousands and have very few followers and only post links. It is very pointless if they have very few followers, but for some reason they do still do it.

@zemote: non-spam tweets a user is involved in the conversation, but only occasionally does self-promotion

@latarahamying: tweet spam is when someone says "take a look at my pics" or when they tell you "hey you can make so and so $$ today"

@StacieBennett: Not sure on definition, but to me when EVERY tweet is 'new blog post' or 'check out my blog' etc. Talk about something else, lol

@mfartr: I think it's a volume issue not a content issue. If all sum1 does is send updates bout self it's spam, mix it up, contribute. and promoting affiliate products is definitely spam

@singlewahm: You were asking what constitutes Twitter spam. Here's a good example. http://twitter.com/askmichaelcurry

So there you have it! If you want to build a solid following at Twitter, you should "tweet" a good mix of: conversation, news, reviews, feedback, tips, relevant information, resources and ideas.

And of course we should mention the cautions: don't be too self-promotional, boring, arrogant, ignore people or have one-sided conversations.

Of course, it's not about building the largest following you can. It's about **attracting** the type of people you want to communicate with. Twitter provides a great platform for building relationships with influencers in your industry, and your target market, all in one convenient place.

Know your objective. Know who you want to meet, and who you want to meet you. Know how you want to be known, and what you want to be known for. And keep at least 90% of your tweets working in that direction.

Your goal may or not be to get on the top 100 hundred most popular Tweeters list. It was a goal of mine, and the day I got on the list, was the day I celebrated and decided a book needed to be written to share how I did it.

Check out who is #100 – hey – at least I got on the list – right? LOL

NOTE: There are a variety of bots on this list. Do not just follow someone because they are on the list. My "rule of thumb" for following people, is when they're in an actual conversation with friends I'm already following, or if they send me an intelligent tweet @ my username.

Check every tweeter out who you follow to make sure they're follow-worthy for your stream and social networking purposes.

The top 100 (or so) most popular

kevinrose (42,839)	woot (9,127)	missrogue (5,804)	enjutomojamuto (4,260)
leolaporte (42,570)	zefrank (9,048)	springnet (5,752)	nick (4,236)
BarackObama (38,300)	darthvader (8,614)	simplebits (5,722)	pistachio (4,208)
JasonCalacanis (27,850)	jowyang (8,324)	acedtect (5,643)	arielwaldman (4,195)
alexalbrecht (27,812)	mashable (8,170)	StephenTColbert (5,556)	hiliaryclinton (4,166)
scobleizer (26,948)	loiclemeur (8,134)	BreakingNewsOn (5,243)	nishio (4,143)
Veronica (24,932)	WilHarris (7,817)	om (5,237)	waynesutton (4,102)
macrumors (23,107)	HenryRollins (7,724)	revision3 (5,163)	rafe (4,003)
THErealDVORAK (22,573)	TUAW (7,576)	Maggie (5,143)	pop17 (3,968)
twitter (21,398)	mollywood (7,557)	cwgabriel (5,014)	startupmeme (3,919)
hotdogsladies (21,236)	sjmcloughlin (7,446)	emilychang (4,958)	cnn (3,795)
MarsPhoenix (20,091)	jkottke (7,151)	johnedwards (4,950)	techmeme (3,604)
techcrunch (19,233)	TwitPic (7,073)	jeffpulver (4,927)	dannysullivan (3,568)
ljustine (16,059)	jeffcannata (7,064)	CNETNews (4,927)	stoweboyd (3,530)
CaliLewis (14,239)	DannyTRS (7,052)	anildash (4,902)	obamanews (3,469)
Twitterrific (14,093)	steverubel (7,036)	digg (4,866)	dough (3,352)
ev (13,856)	problogger (6,909)	fredwilson (4,835)	Hamachiya2 (3,341)
guykawasaki (13,672)	wordpress (6,899)	cc_chapman (4,811)	otsune (3,309)
chrispirillo (12,767)	UstreamTV (6,797)	leahculver (4,781)	drtiki (3,285)
jakemarsh (12,582)	diprager (6,707)	aglick35 (4,771)	snookca (3,098)
ambermacarthur (12,162)	newmediajim (6,658)	sarahlane (4,877)	centernetworks (3,051)
twitlive (12,017)	macworld (6,652)	Zadi (4,674)	armano (3,042)
laughingsquid (11,933)	technorati (6,552)	microformats (4,656)	queenofspain (3,035)
wilw (11,910)	zappos (6,485)	photomatt (4,602)	193Bmedia (2,983)
biz (11,697)	zeldman (6,358)	Mickipedia (4,573)	juliaroy (2,977)
patricknorton (11,415)	damiano (6,306)	kentnichols (4,561)	vpieters (2,843)
bloggersblog (11,288)	SethGodin (6,298)	warrenellis (4,424)	danraine (2,761)
dooce (11,203)	timoreilly (6,278)	t (4,373)	earcos (2,706)
gruber (11,150)	xenijardin (6,098)	borat (4,361)	MaryHodder (2,649)
StephenColbert (10,943)	jack (6,042)	Ed_Dale (4,315)	thegizwiz (2,588)
davewiner (10,206)	juancarzola (5,933)	tradingnothing (4,306)	andybeal (2,546)
garyvee (9,888)	Jmcoon (5,917)	nytimes (4,284)	twitbin (2,542)
chrisbrogan (9,132)	adamcurry (5,815)	joi (4,262)	coachdeb (2,541)

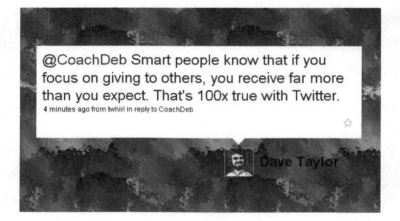

Chapter 6

To Tweet or Not To Tweet

If you are thinking to yourself:

> "Why should I join Twitter and Tweet? What a waste of time!"

You are not alone.

Dozens of internet marketers have publicly stated from stage and in teleseminars saying, *"Twitter is a waste of time and is a total distraction."*

In fact, someone just reported this via a tweet while she was participating at an internet marketing conference in the US just a few minutes ago as this chapter is being written.

But here's where we are torn.

We almost *don't want to* convince them of the power of Twitter. Internet's brief history has shown us what happens when MLMers, internet marketers, or sales people who are only interested in making a buck with whatever tool they get their hands on, do once they have access to that tool.

We have seen what they will do to the blogosphere once they see money making ways to exploit a tool.

And the beauty of Twitter as it is right now is there is a collective group of brilliant minds sharing ideas, resources, tips, and connections so that it's a really nice place to network as it stands.

Once someone uses it for marketing purposes ONLY to make money, they'll ruin the very beauty that is Twitter.

Now if Twitter has been presented to you in the way it was to me, as a silly way to talk about what you had for breakfast every morning, I agree. Waste of time. I had the same reaction at first, and I think every serious entrepreneur has had this feeling at one point or another.

But to stop your mind right there is doing yourself a serious disservice to realizing that the world is changing and mobile marketing is the trend of the future. If you don't catch on now, you'll be crushed by the wave that IS coming in like a Tsuami— just like blogging did in the 90's that internet marketers also mocked when they didn't understand the power behind the tool.

To say Twitter is a waste of time, is to say ALL networking, PR, marketing, advertising and branding is a waste of time.

Think about it.

When's the last time you went to an in-person networking event, conference or meeting?

It could be argued that all of the above are bigger wastes of time when compared to networking, marketing and brand building on Twitter.

Have you ever tracked just how much time is spent going to in-person events? The time it takes for you to shower, shave, dress, put make up on and do your hair before you're presentable to leave the house. (Feel free to @CoachDeb me if you're a bald man who gets to save 30+ minutes every day by being able to skip those last two daily activities for most.)

Then you've got to drive or take public transportation (which takes even longer) to get where you're going, fill up, then spend

90 minutes on the official part of any networking event if there's a luncheon or speaker, then do your meet and greet, and hop back in your car to head back home. Whew! It is exhausting just to read the breakdown of all the time involved in going to in person networking events.

Not to mention if this event is out of town where you have to fly! OMG! Fagedaboudit! Arriving two hours early to catch a flight, going through those annoying security points where they pat down grandma in front of you who forgot she couldn't pack her lotions and potions larger than two ounces. Oi!

Yet these business travelers are often the first to put down Twitter as a "waste of time." Yeah... uh... okay...

New Media & Internet Marketing Secret Revealed:

It's natural that the gurus in the internet marketing world do NOT want you to get on Twitter. After all, Twitter *equalizes* the playing field. Anyone can build a list on Twitter if they do just one thing: participate.

It's the same fear elite media had about bloggers.

All of a sudden, they are no longer the high priests dispelling hidden secrets and information that only they are privy to. Now **the people** have their own Bibles, and they know how to read them and make use of them.

Internet marketers beware of "old thinking" that was popular in the 90's! It's not the way to market online any longer and it's not the trend of the future. There's a whole new way to market online in the 21st century using new media, now often referred to as "social media."

Embrace new media, social media, or whatever buzz word they want to call Web 2.0 these days, and you'll thrive in this new media landscape.

Turn the pages and you'll quickly discover new ways to do business and market online.

PART TWO
SUCCESS ON TWITTER

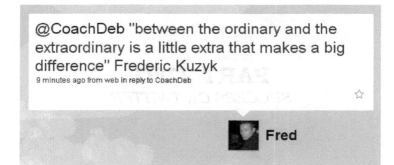

Chapter 7

Top 10 Reasons Companies Need to Tweet

Communication

Robert Scoble, @Scobleizer follows 20K tweeters, Friend Feeders & Gtalk users and is able to stay on top of world news and trends and resources in a way that has never been possible or available to the common business professional without having to invest tens of thousands of dollars on focus groups to get that type of information.

You get instant, quick connection with Twitter. This is important when you want to keep in touch with your Tribe of clients, friends or constituents, and see what they're doing. If your client / follower needs a pick-me-up, motivation or a resourceful tip here and there, you can communicate with them directly through their cell phone or online in seconds.

Brand Recognition

The more you are "top of mind" in your clients or prospects mind, the more you'll be contacted when they need your products or services. The easier you make it for your clients to remember what you do through your username, and remember your name – the better it is for attracting clients on Twitter.

You can also use www.Search.Twitter.com to track and monitor your brand online. You type in your username and it will show all the conversations not only to you but also *about you*. This is where you'll find people talking about you when they didn't send you an @ reply, (meaning the @ symbol wasn't at the beginning of their tweet.) You don't see those messages in your replies tab if they don't have that @ symbol at the beginning of their Tweet, but you will find them on www.Search.Twitter.com.

Reputation Management

Companies are now starting to understand the power of Twitter, and what is also being called micro-blogging. They understand that if they don't have a strong online presence and if they're not on Twitter, their brand could be getting trashed and they wouldn't know it.

I highly recommend you use some type of Google Analytics and Google Alerts tool in order to track your name on the internet. You can also do this through Search.Twitter.com to specifically see what's being tweeted about you, your company and or your brand username on Twitter. You want to make sure that you're tracking your company name or brand and engaging in the conversation.

@AndyBeal wrote an excellent book we highly recommend, "Radically Transparent" that will help you navigate this new world of online brand and reputation management.

Build Your Network of Friends, Colleagues and JV partners

This book is the result of strengthened connections between two business professionals. Warren and Deborah first connected on MySpace.com, but it wasn't until we were both on Twitter that we connected regularly and used the tool to coordinate a business deal.

Coach Deb tweeted her followers on Twitter to follow Warren through a series of tweets saying, "Warren was a legend in the book publishing world, and any of my internet marketing friends who were booking me for speaking gigs told me I should talk to Warren Whitlock when my first book on new media got published." But I've never been one to pick up the phone and call a complete stranger without at least first meeting them somewhere so they'd know I wasn't some crazy stalker or groupie."

We finally met in person at the WIMME conference in San Francisco (WIMME – World Internet Marketing Main Event). Since we already had met online, it was very easy to strike up a conversation and get to know one another even better now that we were face to face.

We talked about everything from business to life. But then, as with any conference, you go back home, back to the office, back to your normal routine, and never really get a chance to connect again quite like you did in person. Then along came Facebook. We added each other as friends there too. But it wasn't until Twitter came on the scene that we not only really got to know each other better but were able to stay in constant connection throughout the day through our tweets.

We were both continually "top of mind" for each other. Until one day... Warren tweeted saying,

@CoachDeb Hey Deb whadda ya' say we write a book together about the power of Twitter?

To which Deborah replied,

@WarrenWhitlock Sounds like a plan! Hey – let's write the book about Twitter ON Twitter so the Twitterverse can contribute!

And the rest... as they say... is history! We continued the conversation via DM (Direct Message) on Twitter, and then took it to IM (instant messenger via Gtalk – google talk).

Attract New Clients

Would you say that most marketers think this should be number one?

The problem with that type of thinking is that if companies focus exclusively on "getting clients" instead of "attracting clients" using permission based marketing, a strategy discussed in detail by best-selling author Seth Godin in his book, "Permission Marketing" they'll miss out on the larger picture of using Twitter to grow their business.

Permission based marketing is the beauty of Twitter, because you end up subtly and persuasively attracting your clients as opposed to chasing them. This is the biggest difference between marketing on Twitter versus traditional and email marketing. It's a 180-degree turn.

It's not the number-one reason we're on Twitter, and it shouldn't be for you either. If it is, people will smell you out, recognize you as a marketplace molester, and think you're just there to get them to become your client. When that happens, they simply unfollow you, and your communication with them comes to a screeching halt.

The beauty of Twitter is you can also unfollow a person and disallow them from sending a direct message if they're just going to use Twitter to spam you with unwanted messages. You can also block people if they just send you sales messages.

The same is true for your tribe of followers. At any moment, they can unfollow you if they feel you're solely using Twitter to send them ads.

The power is in the people's hands on Twitter.

The jobs and clients will come. Trust us. It's okay to go after them. The ideal way to do that however is "off Twitter" or at least off the public channel. This is when direct messages come into play, or chats using Ustream or online chat that you invite people to on Twitter and then go to a different medium.

Deborah got a speaking gig on the Big Island because she tracks **"Hawaii"** on her cell phone and saw that @AndyBeal and @DaveTaylor were hosting a social media summit right there in Hawaii where she lives. She got the gig five days after connecting with them on Twitter.

Business will come. You just need to respect Twitter and its power to make powerful connections.

Find and Connect with Influencers and Keep in Touch

Coach Deb met people like @DaveTaylor and @AndyBeal and @eMom at Blog World Expo in Vegas, but wasn't able to really connect with them on a regular basis – until getting more active on Twitter.

Think about the Twitter revolution this way; when you send an email, it's so easy to ignore it. There's no picture. It's boring old text. You get busy. You don't have time to send dozens of long-winded, personal emails, but on Twitter, you're limited to 140 characters so it's easy and acceptable to connect with 100's of people using your Twitter account since brevity is the norm.

Twitter is a PR agent's dream. Anybody who has ever done PR loves the 140 character limit. You can stay in touch with people very quickly, and not get too wordy.

Search Engine Optimization

Twitter is one of the top SEO (search engine optimization) tools online.

But don't take our word for it. See for yourself.

Go ahead and do a Google search for: CoachDeb and see what comes up. Next do a search for WarrenWhitlock and see what comes up.

If you're looking to be found online, Twitter is an easy way to accomplish this goal, and drive more traffic to your blog or Web site.

The evidence to support how powerful Twitter is in regards to SEO is the overwhelming number of applications (apps) created to track the conversations, subject matter and words that are being talked about.

We created a table full of apps created for Twitter and came up with over seven pages of apps. You'll find this list in a later chapter in this book.

Trend spotting

If you go to www.TweetScan.com, or http://www.twitscoop.com you'll see all of the current conversations happening this very moment. It will show you a tweet cloud. The conversations that are happening and the words that are being most talked about will be bigger and bolder.

Search.Twitter.com is another popular way to track trends being discussed on Twitter all over the world.

Currently the biggest conversation that is being discussed right now is Obama and McCain. This is a topic that will more than likely continue to be in the top ten trending topics for the next several months due to the political elections taking place this year in the United States of America. iPhone is another very popular subject, Olympics and the #DontGo movement have all been top trends and topics for the past month.

When you want to connect with your tribe and find out what they and a lot of other people are talking about, you can also go to www.Twemes.com to see what people are talking about right at this very moment.

All you need to do in order to get in the conversation and appear on Twemes is put a simple little # symbol in front of the word or abbreviation. It's called a hash tag.

(Note: Twemes has recently been having tracking/communication problems ever since Twitter limited their API, however we're hoping they will get things back up to normal, as it was such a resourceful tracking tool for Twitter users.)

Focus groups

Before social networking sites like Twitter were formed, the small business owner was limited in the amount of research he or she could do based on his or her budget.

Most entrepreneurs starting out rarely can invest ten thousand dollars (or more) on a focus group organized to give them feedback on their products or services.

Before Twitter, Focus Groups were reserved for the large corporations with large budgets to invest on advertising and research to get them feedback before they launched a new product line.

Now, anyone can get immediate feedback on their ideas, products and services with a simple 140 tweet that starts with the word POLL in front of it.

Keep in mind, people love to share their feedback, offer their two cents and give their expert opinion on how they feel about a product or service.

And with Twitter, all these people are gathered in one place! The more who actively follow you, the more feedback you'll get.

Whether it's a book like this one, where readers became contributors, or whether it's a new feature for a product you're developing in your company, people like to participate. Let them. Ask them questions. Allow them to give you feedback.

Enhanced conference experience

One of the most powerful ways Twitter is being used is at business conferences.

Let's face it. Entrepreneurs and business professionals need constant intellectual stimulation, or they'll get bored. They're constantly mult-tasking throughout their day. And when they're attending a business conference, they're checking email, the internet, stats, etc.

If the speaker on stage loses their attention, they focus on something more important. Now when you're at an event, you no longer need to wait to begin your networking until the five minute break they give you. Instead, you can simply track the event through your mobile phone or the internet using Twitter and the search apps created to support this activity.

You can hear what anyone in the room thinks about a subject matter simply by following and using the conference abbreviation hashtag. Let's give you an example.

One of the most popular conference events where Twitter is actively used to connect with others at the 2-3,000 attendee conference is SXSW (South By South West).

The hashtag for this event was #SXSW and in order to see all the tweets by attendees at the event – whether you were following them or not – was by sending 'Track SXSW' from your mobile phone via text to Twitter. Or by going to Search.Twitter.com via the internet on your phone or laptop, and searching for 'SXSW' to see what everyone is saying from the conference itself.

If you're having an event in your business that you want to create buzz about, simply announce to your attendees at the beginning of the event what the hashtag is for your event.

TIP: Make your hashtag original. Otherwise, you'll see irrelevant tweets in the stream that have nothing to do with your event. We saw evidence of this at a recent conference titled "IMPACT" and unfortunately, anytime anyone tweeted anything with the word "impact" in it, the tweet would be included in the search you were tracking. By simply adding the year to your hashtag, making it "IMPACT08" you narrow down the tweets you'll see to the actual people at the same event, or following it from the comfort of their home or office.

This is where you'll start seeing the beauty of Twitter in making new connections. You'll find all of the people who are at the conference scheduling "tweetups" in person meetings (or parties) where people from the conference gather after the event is over.

I love Twitter :) I ask and get an outpouring of help! Thank you all SO much. Love you guys, seriously.
about 4 hours ago from web

DonnaFox

Chapter 8

101 Reasons to Tweet

Let's demonstrate the power of Twitter and online social networking by using this chapter in such a way where you can begin to experience the Twitterverse and the power of the blogosphere for yourself. Shall we?

In this printed book, we've shared the **TOP 10 Business Reasons** you need to Tweet.

Now, it's YOUR turn to contribute and be a part of this book – online!

This is what we call an "iChapter" (interactive Chapter) where we start the chapter off here, and you finish it online with additional reasons and ways people Tweet and use online social networks.

It's a new way of writing books – interactively. Thus the "I" standing for interactive, because the knowledge doesn't stop here. You'll continue to expand your mind and learn from many different people on their perspectives on how, what and why people tweet.

To add your two cents on reasons why you tweet, go to:
http://TwitterHandbook.com/blog/101

Hey, you might discover a new way to market online and use mobile marketing for your brand or business simply by seeing another business owner's strategy for using Twitter in their business!

The moment this book is released and available, we'll send a tweet to our followers on Twitter and ask them to add their reasons to tweet, so you can begin to get so many additional ideas of ways and reasons to use Twitter that you might not ever have thought of on your own.

This way, you can share your expertise and learn from others and get different perspectives other than the authors of this book.

Sound like a plan?

SIDE BENEFIT of this new way of writing a chapter: We trust you'll enjoy this creative way of saving paper, keeping this book shorter than a 1,000 page text book of which it could become, all while keeping you updated with the most up to date content and trends on Twitter by you taking advantage of up to date blogs and comments from users themselves.

Let's get the list started based on the tweets we've received, and trends we've observed during our time on Twitter...

1. Twitter combats loneliness – in an age where we're so busy with our lives, businesses and transient lifestyle, many solo business owners who spend 90% of their day locked up in their offices are now turning to Twitter to get inspired from other like-minded people – regardless of their geographical location.

2. Kill the boredom when standing online – no longer do you need to be impatient when standing on a long line during the holidays. Instead, be sure to have your mobile phone with you, tuned in to Twitter so you can participate in the conversation and share a little about what you're up to while you're (patiently) waiting in line.

3. Twitter is easy to use when traveling – You can tweet from your mobile phone which gives you fast communication to all the people you know who are following you so you can get help or information when you need it, or share what you're up to so we can live vicariously through you for a moment.

4. Twitter gives you instant access to thousands of people from your cell phone just by hitting the send button via text messaging

5. Twitter allows you to keep your cell phone number private yet still communicate with your tribe of clients, subscribers and following

6. Twitter gives you the ability to connect with people of diverse backgrounds, countries, areas and opinions, giving you access to a wealth of knowledge on any given subject

7. You can outsource your memory to Twitter - next time you forget something – just tweet the question and watch how quickly your memory gets jogged with the answers you'll get!

8. Remember The Milk is an app that husbands are using to stay out of the dog house

9. Jott.com and Utterz.com allows you to communicate with your tribe using voice

10. Fast communication – with 140 character limits your clients, followers and business associates are forced to Get to the POINT and not waste a lot of your precious time

11. Fast response time – you can instantly connect with people and communicate in real time – without any cost – provided you're using the internet or have unlimited text messaging service from your mobile phone

12. Instantly thank people for a meeting you just had without before even getting back to the office, or flight home

13. Get smarter by asking a tech question – a bazillion of brilliant geeks are ready to answer your question, problem or dilemma – getting resolution faster than any type of HELP service on the net from "tech support"

14. Follow the trends by following a lot of people

15. Become "top of mind" in the minds of your customers and prospects by daily tweeting intriguiging tweets getting them to like you more and more with each tweet.

Now it's YOUR turn to share the reasons why YOU tweet online at:

http://TwitterHandbook.com/blog/101

Join the Twibe & get smarter!

@CoachDeb Marketing is discovering how to solve someone else's deepest pain...then letting them know you're there.

6 minutes ago from twhirl in reply to CoachDeb

 Jonathan Fields

Chapter 9

Twitter Success Stories in the Real World

Success Stories - Real People Using Twitter with Real Results

Missing Woman Found

Just before Thanksgiving of 2007, Chris Wilson's (@aithene) sister-in-law went missing. When the case stalled out with the Florida police, the family started looking for other means of finding her. As a web designer and new media hobbyist, Chris used the skills he had and started a Wordpress Blog with all of the details, and then turned to his Twitter Network.

Chris told his story:

> "We were unsure what anyone could do, since this was MY network, not my sister-in-law's, but we put the call out there, figuring that if nothing else, we might generate some diggs and try to get some media attention and coverage to help out the search.

> "What really ended up happening, though, was that it made my twitter network aware of what I was going thru,

and this awareness began shaping things in a very unexpected way. It became a truly mind-opening experience for me.

"Dozens of knowledgeable folks began offering advice on where to look, who to call, what needed to be done, and what information still needed to be gathered. Many of these were people who had lost friends and family in a similar way and who had experience with the ins and outs of a missing-person search.

"See, I didn't approach a network of people who had been involved with missing people, but one immediately formed around me. They provided information that my family didn't have and that wasn't provided by law enforcement. The police, in fact, offered very little in the way of advice on what we could do. They opened a case, told us they were looking, and then after they determined that she'd left the state, kind of quit. So, having recommendations come from people who have gone through all of this before was priceless.

"One grand Kudos goes to Christopher Penn (@cspenn) who provided a real turning point in our search efforts. Because of Chris' marketing background, he is VERY well versed with MySpace. Since Manessa's social network lived on MySpace, Chris volunteered his time and expertise to set up a MySpace page and invited all of Manessa's online network to help join us in searching for her, then turned the keys over to us to manage. This was something that no one in our family really knew about, and we might have ended up waiting for days before it happened if left to us. Immediately after this site was up, however, we began receiving all sorts of information. We knew what state she was in, we knew what friends she'd been hanging around with, and we had several 'sightings' of her.

"There were also tweeters who offered time and support in other ways, all of which were appreciated. In the end, this group of friends and colleagues that I had hoped MIGHT act as a small Digg army (which they did very well, by the way) and possibly pass along some links, had self-organized around us to create a small, but very knowledgeable task force in a very relevant, but completely unexpected way.

"This was such an unbelievably organic response, it caught my family and I completely off-guard. It gave me another perspective on, and a new respect for something that had beforehand simply been a playground and pass time for me."

One Word Saved His Life

Student James Karl Buck was arrested in Egypt. He sent one-word message using Twitter about his arrest: ARRESTED.

> "On his way to the police station, Buck took out his cell phone and sent a message to his friends and contacts using the micro-blogging site Twitter.

> "The message only had one word. "Arrested."

> "Within seconds, colleagues in the United States and his blogger-friends in Egypt -- the same ones who had taught him the tool only a week earlier -- were alerted that he was being held.

> "Buck was able to send updates every couple of hours saying he was still detained, he had spoken to the prosecutor, he still had not been charged."

CNN covered his story. But tweeters heard about it first on Twitter.

Creation of New Technology

We've been talking to Damon P. Cortesi about his TweetStats app. Great graphs of your twitter usage, or any other user. (One of the best looking Twitter related sites I've seen, fun and useful). Follow this brilliant guy on Twitter @dacort

Damon agreed to an interview for the Twitter Revolution and here it is:

How did you get started using Twitter?
I first signed up in December of 2006 and then my account lay dormant until May of '07 when I got a few friends on it. We're geographically spread out, but would share our daily activities and it was really nice to be able to keep up with my friends. When Twitter introduced the "tracking" feature, my usage skyrocketed as it much easier to find people interested in the same things I was.

What motivated you to create an TweetStat?
I was just about to post my 2000th update and was curious how I had been using Twitter over that time and who I had been talking to. A couple hours and a perl script later, I had some charts that displayed my usage. Once I posted a screenshot of that, I found that others were interested in quantifying their Twitter usage but the script I released was limited to those familiar with perl on OS X with iWork Numbers. I took the opportunity to learn Ruby on Rails and make a web service that everybody could use.

What results have you seen from twitter use (and the app)?
Twitter has expanded my social circle, introducing me to people not only in my hometown of Seattle, but also across the world. For example, I met up with a fellow Tweeter in Amsterdam when I was there for a conference. We had never met in person before, but organized via Twitter, had a couple beers and some interesting conversation. It also allows me to keep in touch with my good friends in a way I hadn't been able to previously - I'm horrible at keeping in touch. I think TweetStats introduced me

to a number of people I wouldn't have met otherwise. Much to the chagrin of some of my followers who are close friends in real life, I then started tweeting like crazy.

What's planned for the future?
I hope to continue to provide even more useful information with TweetStats. Right now it's a site that's kind of fun, but is definitely lacking a definitive usefulness. While it's great to be able to quantify your Twitter activity, I'd really love to dig into the data and provide some practical information to help people analyze their Twitter community in addition to their own activity. Unfortunately, as it's merely a side project for me and as such, new features are generally slow to roll out.

Here are a few graphs to show you what your stats might look like once you start actively tweeting with others:

Twitter Success Stories in the "Real World"

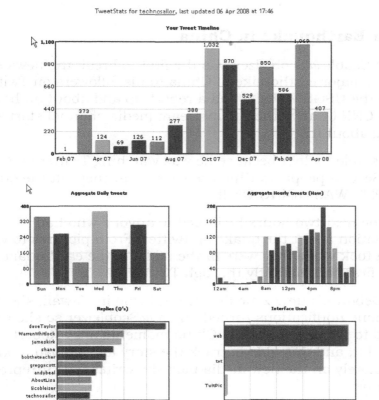

Major Earthquake in China

Robert Scoble @Scobleizer was the first to break the news story about a major earthquake in China to his followers on Twitter before the USGS Website had a report up and about an hour before CNN or any other mainstream media channel started talking about it.

He was able to do it because he was watching Twitter on Google Talk. Several people in China reported that they felt the quake WHILE IT WAS GOING ON!!!

Over the next two hours he linked to anyone who had information about the quake on twitter. From pictures to videos people took while they were in the midst of the earthquake, we saw it first and instantly through Twitter.

With Deborah's time zone difference, living in Hawaii, she had her phone notifications turned on for @Scobleizer so she was alerted to the earthquake in China moments after Robert tweeted it, and was able to track the story and upload a post immediately on the new media blog she writes for Entrepreneur magazine.

Both Deborah and Robert were able to break the news first, before mainstream media channels were able to get to the scene, set up their cameras, and cover the story.

It's amazing the kind of news you can learn by being on Twitter and the connections you can make among people across the world.

Government Alerts

@SharonMcP told us about how she learned of the lights going out in Washington:

> "It was through the tweets of Congressman Culberson (@johnculberson) from the House floor that I first learned of Speaker Nancy Pelosi's efforts to silence the Republican's request for a vote on domestic drilling by turning off the lights, cameras and microphones.
>
> In this instance it was Twitter that reported the news - before the 'news'."

The following pages are from Congressman Culberson's Twitter page sent from his mobile phone from the House floor the day the lights went out in Washington, and C-SPAN had to shut off its broadcast to American TV's, and the firestorm of tweets it started. It was the only news coverage possible to get the word out of what was going on.

> Blogs and social nets yesterday proved the power of new media. Comp coverage, accurate too, where C-SPAN/cable/MSM news couldn't go. Awesome
> 05:07 AM August 02, 2008 from TwitterBerry

This was the beginning of the Twitter Revolution that went on for the following week with #DontGo as the #1 trending topic on Search.Twitter.com, and continues to this day.

@fnamelname It's been pretty amazing...social media is really helping drive a political event. Coverage is everywhere. #dontgo (forgot hash)
28 minutes ago from web in reply to fnamelname

Andrew Wright

johnculberson

▸ ✓**Following** ✓Device updates ON

Good night all!

about 5 hours ago from web ☆

@CoachDeb Got it - thanks about 5 hours ago from web in reply to CoachDeb ☆

@JosephTX #tx7 I just watched the women's gymnastics - one of my favorites. US team almost won the gold but a few bad slips & we won silver about 5 hours ago ☆ from web in reply to JosephTX

@CoachDeb No but I will tell them Friday - where can I see trending topics? about 5 hours ago from web in reply to CoachDeb ☆

@CoachDeb Yes - Sunlight of social media is the best hope for We the People to regain control over our elected officials & our government about 5 hours ago ★ from web in reply to CoachDeb

@CoachDeb Imagine a day vry soon when I can tweet #tx7 to over 100,000 of my constituents for a quick legis action alert, a poll or convers about 5 hours ago ★ from web in reply to CoachDeb

@skamphax0r TY! about 5 hours ago from web in reply to skamphax0r ☆

@TheWebPixie No west and southwest Houston District 7 - George HW Bush 1st Congressman, 1967-71, then Bill Archer, 1971-2001, then me about 5 hours ago ☆ from web in reply to TheWebPixie

@mojosd Yes you are welcome to call me at 713 682 8828 about 5 hours ago from ☆ web in reply to mojosd

@technosailor It works for every district in the country - another selling point for me to pursuade colleagues they need to be on Twitter! about 6 hours ago from web ☆ in reply to technosailor

@CoachDeb Yes the tidal force of the internet community & common sense &

Twitter Success Stories in the "Real World"

@technosailor It works for every district in the country - another selling point for me to pursuade colleagues they need to be on Twitter! about 6 hours ago from web in reply to technosailor ☆

@CoachDeb Yes the tidal force of the internet community & common sense & 70% of public is bearing down on her & she is starting to fold about 6 hours ago from web in reply to CoachDeb ☆

@JosephTX Thanks Joseph! Encourage CD7 residents to use #tx7 in their posts to me so I can single them out - old media gets older every day about 6 hours ago from web in reply to JosephTX ☆

@engagejoe TYI about 6 hours ago from web in reply to engagejoe ☆

@Obscura Cong Ted Poe is #tx2 - he is one of my best friends & he & I are usually right in the middle of stirring things up on the floor about 6 hours ago from web in reply to Obscura ☆

@phelina You are the first District 7 constit to use #tx7 - congrats! - I am convinced this is the future for all elected officials about 6 hours ago from web in reply to nmoneypenny ☆

@phelina #tx7 Thank you! I will send out blast emails to my large lists w instructions on Twitter & #tx7 & ask for retweets to tx7 residents about 6 hours ago from web in reply to nmoneypenny ☆

@hunterligon Yes Mary was there on the first day w me - and thanks for the kind words! about 6 hours ago from web in reply to hunterligon ☆

@technosailor Today I figured out how to zero in on my constituents for conversations if we use #tx7. It works for all districts examp: #ca9 about 6 hours ago from web in reply to technosailor ☆

@technosailor I knew it was coming up but that's too far out yet for me to zero in on it - about 6 hours ago from web in reply to technosailor ☆

@MaryTrigiani Maybe Dana Roherbacher - Cong Pete Hoekstra & I & Cong Mike Burgess are posting here personally with no staff about 6 hours ago from web in reply to MaryTrigiani ☆

Here is the Search.Twitter.com stream where we were able to communicate with Congressman Culberson despite not having his phone number or ever having met him – all through Twitter from his mobile phone to ours:

CoachDeb: @johnculberson do your friends on The Hill know that #dontgo was #1 trending topic on twitter 4 entire week?
about 3 hours ago · Reply · View Tweet · Show Conversation

johnculberson: @CoachDeb Yes - Sunlight of social media is the best hope for We the People to regain control over our elected officials & our government
about 3 hours ago · Reply · View Tweet · Show Conversation

johnculberson: @CoachDeb Imagine a day vry soon when I can tweet #tx7 to over 100,000 of my constituents for a quick legis action alert, a poll or convers
about 3 hours ago · Reply · View Tweet · Show Conversation

CoachDeb: @johnculberson its a true revolution happening right b4 our very eyes! May I quote u4 The Twitter Handbook I'm writing 2 be published th ...
about 3 hours ago · Reply · View Tweet · Show Conversation

johnculberson: @CoachDeb Yes the tidal force of the internet community & common sense & 70% of public is bearing down on her & she is starting to fold
about 4 hours ago · Reply · View Tweet · Show Conversation

CoachDeb: @johnculberson did my tweetin ears hear correctly? Pelosi mite "let" our govt vote on #dontgo ? Keep up the good fight! #DHDN !
about 4 hours ago · Reply · View Tweet · Show Conversation

WarrenWhitlock: @CoachDeb #NME will be the last chance for pre-book release Twinterviews. Then BIG TIME promo for #BWE with you as the Rock Star
about 4 hours ago · Reply · View Tweet · Show Conversation

Page 1 » Older

E_Wall: #dontgo It's pretty cool being involved with Twitter history. Why has the US not built any new refineries in 25 years?
about 3 hours ago · Reply · View Tweet

Twitter Success Stories in the "Real World"

twitter | coachdeb | Search |

Realtime results for coachdeb   0.09 seconds

politicians: GOP Rep johnculberson: @CoachDeb Got it - thanks
http://tinyurl.com/6z8k3f (expand)
about 3 hours ago · Reply · View Tweet

politicians: GOP Rep johnculberson: @CoachDeb No but I will tell them Friday -
where can I see trending top.. http://tinyurl.com/5rrcq5 (expand)
about 3 hours ago · Reply · View Tweet

politicians: GOP Rep johnculberson: @CoachDeb Yes - Sunlight of social media is
the best hope for We the Pe.. http://tinyurl.com/5q2yy3 (expand)
about 3 hours ago · Reply · View Tweet

johnculberson: @**CoachDeb** Got it - thanks
about 3 hours ago · Reply · View Tweet · Show Conversation

CoachDeb: @johnculberson when u enter dontgo in search box you'll see all the
peeps tweetin about #dontgo movement & column shows top 10 trending ...
about 3 hours ago · Reply · View Tweet · Show Conversation

CoachDeb: @johnculberson 2 see trending topics go 2 http://Search.Twitter.com
under search box you'll see what peeps talking about
about 3 hours ago · Reply · View Tweet · Show Conversation

johnculberson: @**CoachDeb** No but I will tell them Friday - where can I see
trending topics?

> **johnculberson:** **@CoachDeb** Got it - thanks
> about 3 hours ago · Reply · View Tweet · 💬 Show Conversation

> **CoachDeb:** @johnculberson when u enter dontgo in search box you'll see all the peeps tweetin about #dontgo movement & column shows top 10 trending ...
> about 3 hours ago · Reply · View Tweet · 💬 Show Conversation

> **CoachDeb:** @johnculberson 2 see trending topics go 2 http://Search.Twitter.com under search box you'll see what peeps talking about
> about 3 hours ago · Reply · View Tweet · 💬 Show Conversation

> **johnculberson:** **@CoachDeb** No but I will tell them Friday - where can I see trending topics?
> about 3 hours ago · Reply · View Tweet · 💬 Show Conversation

> **downtheticket:** @johnculberson **@CoachDeb** You're both doing great work. Keep up the pressure!
> about 3 hours ago · Reply · View Tweet

> **CoachDeb:** @johnculberson do your friends on The Hill know that #dontgo was #1 trending topic on twitter 4 entire week?
> about 3 hours ago · Reply · View Tweet · 💬 Show Conversation

> **johnculberson:** **@CoachDeb** Yes - Sunlight of social media is the best hope for We the People to regain control over our elected officials & our government
> about 3 hours ago · Reply · View Tweet · 💬 Show Conversation

> **johnculberson:** @CoachDeb Imagine a day vry soon when I can tweet #tx7 to over 100,000 of my constituents for a quick legis action alert, a poll or convers
> about 3 hours ago · Reply · View Tweet · 💬 Show Conversation

Once mainstream media got a hold of this story, we began to see opponents of the #DontGo Movement begin to spam the twitterstream and #dontgo hashtag.

When we say spam, we mean when someone tweets the following "poopies #dontgo" just to clog up the stream for anyone trying to follow the conversation, debate or news of what's going on.

Debate on Twitter is always welcome, but if you don't have anything intelligent to share other than arbitrary words that don't contribute to the conversation, it's considered spam, and only makes the spammer look silly. More on this in another chapter.

This goes for presidential elections or any other topic or conference that's making the top 10 trending topics.

If you simply tweet the name of the hashtag, you'll look like you have nothing interesting to contribute and won't gain followers.

Think of something valuable contribute, whether it's an argument or agreement, it doesn't matter. Just think "provide value" otherwise you'll simply look silly.

Ahh... liberals #dontgo spamming our feed for very long. When you want to join the debate and stop hurling Twitter poop, let us know. about 2 hours ago from web

Republicans want solutions to high gas prices and Democrats offer Twitter poop. Who would you choose? #dontgo about 3 hours ago from web

@davidjhinson So are you in Orlando now? Hope the move has gone/is going well! about 8 hours ago from web in reply to davidjhinson

If you have other #dontgo resources to link to on http://dontgo.us, DM me. Of course, http://dontgomovement.com will likely launch today too about 8 hours ago from web

allenfuller

› ✓Following

@jowyang You should to to the Hill and follow the #dontgo movement. It's really extraordinary. Congressmen on Qik? Crazy!

about 1 hour ago from web in reply to jowyang

@afightingfaith most Americans prefer to have greater mobility than just the distance we can walk in a day. leave the dark ages in the past about 5 hours ago from web in reply to afightingfaith

@afightingfaith glad your car runs on rainbows and unicorns, but most of ours need gas. #dontgo about 5 hours ago from web in reply to afightingfaith

Business Opportunities through Twitter

Patti Serrano tells us how she has used Twitter as a tool for meeting business associates, talking to co-producers and just overall fun.

"I have had Tweetups and started business relationships from Twitter followers. From my Online Spanish classes...@LaGringa I have gained students wanting to learn Spanish by tweeting the classes were about to start. @BeckyMcCray was one of them.

From my zany, wacky, everyone thinks Grandma is drunk show,,,,, @CallYourGrandma I have announced to followers I was going ON THE AIR. I call them Grandma Heads and they go to wherever I tweet, either to http://www.ustream.tv or http://www.talkshoe.com and from those tweets I am continually amazed how many pop in because of the tweet.

From my Online Video Magazine @BIMwebTV I tweet all the people who I am interviewing and that badge runs 24/7 on http://www.BIMwebTV.com

From @PATTI_with_an_i have met the most business contacts and fun. My first Tweetup was with the Denver Podcasters where I meet @GoldieKatsu we went on to produce the KosherEating 101 Podcast. I met @RobMcNealy and @KristieMcNealy they came to my BIZ Show and attended one of my events. I met @RonaldLewis @GeekGirlTV @Genuine and many more. Just an incredible experience. From those meetups in Denver, Goldie has asked me to partake in the executive committee of the Thin Air Summit.

Then from a local search @DivinePurposeMV asked me to tweetup with her and @StevieKnight. We met for coffee, it was awesome and now Stevie Is going with me to the next Denver meeting.

@LindaLocke from California has bought my book from a Tweet and from that we formed a informal BIZ relationship. @Caroldc in Dallas and I are in the talking stages about forming an alliance to start Networking Chapters there in conjunction with my Entrepreneur Club. As is, @Maxweb who owns a restaurant in Colorado and wants me to bring my Entrepreneur Club in for a Networking Chapter meeting.

In just a few short months I have made some incredible contacts, not to mention all the fun I have tweeting back and forth. I call it my playground because it is so entertaining, yet very informative. Some of the links people post are just down right amazing. I have never had an experience like this."

Lisa Van Allen also shared with us how she was able to gain business contacts from using Twitter.

"What you're saying about relationship marketing is right on the mark! It's true everywhere, but especially true in the twitterverse. When I posted a few tweets about issues a coaching client was having, it struck a chord with a guy who was experiencing similar struggles. This man was not looking for a coach - but ended up hiring me because of his appreciation for my tweets. I believe I have barely scratched the surface on ways to use twitter in my practice!"

Joe Philipson, a creative photographer in Hawaii, known to all his Flickr.com and Twitter.com friends as @JPhilipson told us how he gets most of his business through people who follow him on Twitter!

Connect With Influencers

@AdamDesAutels tells us about using twitter:

I signed up for Twitter in February 2008. Not knowing anything about the site and not seeing any immediate value in the service, so I let it sit dormant for a month. One day I was killing time and thought I would find some interesting people to follow and gather information about Social Media. The people I followed and the conversations that I watched were amazing! I wanted to get more involved but didn't really know what to say or how to interact.

After a week of following conversations and not getting involved, I watched a video by Gary Vaynerchuk (@garyvee - Host of Wine Library TV and Internet Celebrity) called "Twitter vs Facebook...kinda". I replied to his Tweet giving my thoughts on the two and what happened next changed my life. On March 26, 2008 I received a Twitter "Direct Message" from Gary that read:

"Adam Agreed DUDE Hey you should make a blog post on it, get your voice/thoughts out there! U have a lot to offer!"

I was truly taken back by this message. The fact that someone with about 14,000 followers and a gigantic internet presence would reply to me with a compliment, opened my eyes to how powerful Twitter can be. And, by the way, I did what Gary said and started a blog (www.AdamDesAutels.com). Which I would never had done if it wasn't for that Twitter message.

That was the tipping point, I was hooked! I started adding more interesting people and interacting with them. Then I noticed something I haven't experienced before on any other Social Network... I was rubbing shoulders with some major internet players. Having conversations with founders and executives of major internet start-ups, making international business contacts, and having a ton of fun.

From the time I joined Twitter I have met and interacted with people that were previously unreachable and made some lifetime connections (business and personal). My name is Adam DesAutels and I am a Twitaholic!

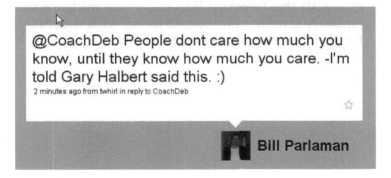

@CoachDeb People dont care how much you know, until they know how much you care. -I'm told Gary Halbert said this. :)

2 minutes ago from twhirl in reply to CoachDeb

Bill Parlaman

Meeting New People

Mike Templeton shares how he has met up with people he first met online through Twitter.

> "Twitter has facilitated a lot of new connections for me even in my local area. dmtweetup.org was built in response to Twitter and is now the central hub for tweetups in our area (Central Iowa).
>
> One of the things that has helped us out at our meetups is the use of Tweetup Badges (@tweetupbadges), which are essentially like event badges with the users Twitter handle and their real name. That way, the next time you're walking into a dark and gloomy bar, look for the guy with the Tweetup Badge on and mitigate the embarrassment that comes along with meeting someone for the first time in real life."

Realtors

We're now collecting stories like this one about a Real Estate agent that connected with a local person on Twitter and didn't just say "got a property to list". After joining and getting followers @NRVLiving was able to get new clients.

> "I got a message from @TMarkiewicz that said he and his wife were going to be leaving the area, and they wanted to talk with me about possibly listing their home. WOW ... here was this guy I'd never met who was inviting me into his home to discuss being his representative, and solely because of the relationship I'd formed with him on Twitter. I was floored. We talked, we negotiated, and a few weeks later we listed his home. Suddenly, it happened again. Another message, this time from @stuboo (don't you just love some of these names?). This message was a little different, it said "@NRVLiving, have you ever gotten a client from Twitter?". When I responded yes, he wrote back "would you like another one?"
>
> "Amazing. Two clients, a buyer and a seller, both acquired through relationships formed on Twitter."

Twitter Used in Education

Willis Whitlock wrote the following article on the use of Twitter in education by teachers and students and the impact it has on learning.

Teaching is society's second most private act.

This aphorism expressed the isolation and frustration many teachers felt at the end of the last century. The world of information raged around them, but when the bell would ring, they closed the door to the world and started the days lessons.

Software like Twitter is changing that in some dramatic ways.

EduTweeps (education Twitter people) are a significant number of Twitter users. The benefits of Twitter documented in the rest of this book apply to education in many of the same ways.

Educational technologists, people who promote the use of technology in education, were the first to sign on. They networked and shared on Twitter before many other professions. The practice is quickly spreading to all teachers. History teachers and Science teachers, Math teachers and administrators see the advantages of networking on Twitter. As evidence, a check of Summize shows tweet trends about major education conferences often hit the top 10.

Teachers use Twitter for professional development.

The most popular use for Twitter for EduTweeps is teacher professional development. The Personal Learning Networks (PLN) meme is big in education. The idea of teacher as life long learner responsible for his own development is taking hold. The PLN allows teachers to take control of their Professional Development and seek out like minded teachers.

For many teachers, Twitter is the PLN. Blogs and wikis, Second

Life lectures and live streaming presentations are where the content is. Twitter is n the backbone. Teachers point out resources and encourage each other on Twitter.

EduTweeps have daily immediate access to education technology rock stars @teach42, @dwarlick, @shareski, @stevehargadon, @kathyschrock, and @wfryer. Each has over 1,000 followers. Hundreds more working educators like @langwitches, @kjarrett, @robinellis, and @teachakidd have a few hundred followers. The education network on Twitter is extensive and strong. As @RavenPhoenix tweets "It is the whole instant reach out and touch factor...at any moment, I can pick the brainpower of edus all over!"

PLN activities include:
Conference back channels - the conference within a conference. EduTweeps are in constant connection with others at these events. Tweets range from the topic at hand to where attendees will Tweetup later to discuss the conference.

Sharing training- Trainers and speakers regularly post daily schedules. EduTweeps know how to access a live stream of training or where it will be blogged.

Marketing blogs - Like others, EduTweeps use Twitter to notify new blog posts.

Polls - Twitter helps take the pulse of the community and direct participants to more in depth polls.

Teachers use Twitter with students.

@eclipseempire uses Twitter to update announcements to students, teachers and parents at Granite Hills High School via @GHHS.

@jamielpeters uses Twitter to arrange Skype calls between classes in different parts of the country are coordinated on Twitter. Many just in time solutions to such calls would be impossible with out it.

An eighth grade English teacher in Maryland used Twitter to help his students write a sci-fi novel titled @ManyVoices. The story of a mermaid who becomes human took six weeks and involved over one hundred students living in six different countries. The title comes from the Twitter account the students used to write the book

"It was incredibly simple and really amazing. My students and I would come in, and suddenly kids in China had written a chapter for the book," George Mayo, the teacher, told Education Week. He created the account and invited his students and students around the world to contribute. The book is now available for free download on Lulu or in paperback for $5.95.

Like Mayo, many teachers find that Twitter is a better online collaboration tool than wikis or blogs. Some of the reasons include:

Easy access - Twitter is invisible technology. The student doesn't need to learn a set of buttons and menus.

Low Risk - Reluctant learners can handle 140 characters (usually less). There's little chance of failure.

Real time - Students see their project grow as they work. Collaborators can work from different computers with out fear of clogging the project (a problem with many blogs and wikis)

No formatting - Given bells and whistles, many students will ring and toot instead of write. The simplicity of Twitter offers only a place to add text.

Concise writing - 140 characters means each word has to be necessary. The process of posting to Twitter forces students to become better writers.

The Twitter future of Twitter in education.

"Tweet me your answer to these 10 questions," says the teacher. Students take the brief quiz and the teachers get immediate results. This is bad news for sellers of digital response systems with teacher labor intensive setups and costly proprietary devices. But good news for teachers and students, most of whom already have cell phones to participate.

Twitter Youth has appeared on the scene. The site offers teacher control and a student project focus in a Twitterlike site. It's not quite Twitter but addresses security concerns of schools. More edu-apps developed for Twitter are sure to follow.

Teachers feel the need to teach students in the world they live in. Twitter and services like it will be available for most of students lives. The sooner they learn to use it well, the better.

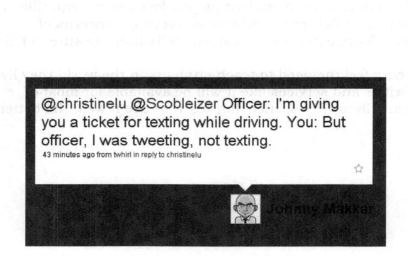

@christinelu @Scobleizer Officer: I'm giving you a ticket for texting while driving. You: But officer, I was tweeting, not texting.

43 minutes ago from twhirl in reply to christinelu

Johnny Makkar

The Twitter Whale

We're sorry but this chapter is experiencing a glitch in the Matrix. Please come back later when it may – or may not – be back up.

Something is technically wrong. Please take a break, stretch, and use this time when you would've been reading or tweeting to get a cup of coffee, jamba juice, slushie or some caramels. We'll be back to you in a moment. Or not... we don't really know. It all depends on whether the whale wants this chapter to continue...

We have a love/hate relationship with "The Twitter Whale". It shows up when Twitter is "down". For early adopters, we began to see the whale way more often than we would've liked in the Spring of 2008.

We'll always remember the Spring of 2008.

There were a number of reasons why whale spottings were all too common, but we're hopeful for the future of Twitter that they'll get their act together, host their service on much better servers then they were in Spring of 2008, and stay stable for all of us who've grown to love and depend on Twitter to stay connected & informed with what's going on in the world, and in the lives or our clients, contacts, friends and family.

The good news about when things go wrong in the techno-verse, is there are more than a few dozen techies who go about and figure out a way to create something to replace Twitter.

Currently, there are many exciting open source projects that are in development and will more than likely be available to the public (or at least a few understanding beta testers) by the time this book goes to print.

This is exciting news! Because regardless of whether you're using Twitter to keep in touch with your clients, fans and followers, via your mobile phone, or something else that's copying the trend Twitter started – we'll all be "tweeting" in one form or another. Whether it's actually ON Twitter – or some other private, independent service that gives us instant access to mass amounts of people.

Twitter started the mobile trend in America. And for that – we'll always love Twitter. Even when the whale shows its ugly head.

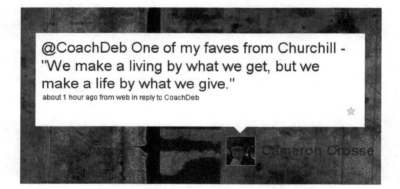

@CoachDeb One of my faves from Churchill -
"We make a living by what we get, but we
make a life by what we give."
about 1 hour ago from web in reply to CoachDeb

Cameron Crosse

Chapter 10

Twitter APPS it's Not Just About Twitter

MarlaBollak

> ✓Following −Device updates OFF

@CoachDeb Twitter is an app. Apps (tools) can talk to (or work with) other applications (tools). Twitter talks to other apps.

about 1 hour ago from web in reply to CoachDeb ☆

@CoachDeb An application (app) is a software program, or tool. A website is an app. A web browser is an app. (more coming...) about 1 hour ago from web in reply to ☆ CoachDeb

Before finishing this chapter on Twitter apps, we figured the best way to ensure we're describing what an "app" is to a non-techie, and do justice to the word to all the "techno-geeks" who know how to create an app, is to tweet about it and ask the Twitterverse if our definition was spot-on.

Turns out we were – but we also got some fantastic responses – immediately back within moments of tweeting out the question.

Ahhhh now do you see why we're so addicted to Twitter?

Here are a few of the immediate @ replies to my 3-tweet question on the definition of a Twitter app:

 wendyybailey: **@CoachDeb** I like it! It's clear, concise and user-friendly. I'm sort of techy and it made gr8 sense to me.
5 minutes ago · Reply · View Tweet

 SharonMcP: **@CoachDeb** course I don't know much about Twitter apps, but I'd say that pretty much describes them.
6 minutes ago · Reply · View Tweet · Show Conversation

 AussieWebmaster: **@coachdeb** you seem to have it right
8 minutes ago · Reply · View Tweet · Show Conversation

 CoachDeb: (cont) the numerous tools, software, add-ons and Web sites devoted to supporting Twitter and other social media technology. (Twitter APPS)
9 minutes ago · Reply · View Tweet

 CoachDeb: What's a Twitter App? App is just a short way to say "application". Twitter Apps is techno-speak jargon used to describe the numerous tools,
10 minutes ago · Reply · View Tweet

 CoachDeb: here's what I've got in the book right now - anyone care to correct me? or revise and make it bettter? (see next 2 tweets)
11 minutes ago · Reply · View Tweet

 CoachDeb: Since i'm not a total techno-geek, I just want to make sure when I describe Twitter APPS in the TWitter Handbook, I'm doing it justice...
11 minutes ago · Reply · View Tweet

(HINT: These tweeters who replied instantly are valuable resources; you may want to consider following them so when you've got a techie question, they'll be there for you like they were there for me.)

Remember, when following the conversation on Twitter (or any type of blog, you go from bottom up to see the original question and then follow the answers to that question.

Twitter APPS it's Not Just About Twitter

 SharonMcP: @CoachDeb "Chief App Watcher for the Twitter Handbook blog"
http://twitterhandbook.com/blog I LIKE that title, thanks Coach.
half a minute ago · Reply · View Tweet · ⤶ Show Conversation

 RickWolff: **@CoachDeb** A Twitter App is a web app that takes Twitter's data and
presents it in a special way.
5 minutes ago · Reply · View Tweet

 affiliatetips: **@CoachDeb** Apps would be anything executable. It runs on your
computer or a server.
half a minute ago · Reply · View Tweet

 wendyybailey: **@CoachDeb** I like it! It's clear, concise and user-friendly. I'm sort of
techy and it made gr8 sense to me.
7 minutes ago · Reply · View Tweet

affiliatetips: **@CoachDeb** Not to be confused with an appliance or applique.
less than a minute ago · Reply · View Tweet · ⤶ Show Conversation

MarlaBollak: **@CoachDeb** An application (app) is a software program, or tool. A
website is an app. A web browser is an app. (more coming…)
22 minutes ago · Reply · View Tweet

Twitter APPS

Apps to enhance your Twitter experience

What's a Twitter App? App is just a short way to say "application". Twitter Apps is techno-speak jargon used to describe the numerous tools, software, add-ons and Web sites devoted to supporting Twitter and other social media technology.

The sheer number of apps being created since the popularity of Twitter can be a time-consuming task in and of itself.

People often ask me how I have time to tweet and do all the things I do on a daily basis. They ask how I manage my time, and what resources or strategies do I rely on to help me get more done in one day than most executives do in a week.

My favorite answer, "I don't sleep."

One of the things I do to keep things organized when I'm on Twitter is when I come across a cool link, resource or app, I copy/paste it into a table so I can revisit it later when I'm in between projects.

This table became incredibly useful when doing research for this book.

But we didn't want to leave it to our own research. Instead, we held the first ever TwitCast Radio Show and asked the Twitterverse to participate and share their favorite app.

This is one of our favorite benefits of using Twitter. **The power to learn more than you could in the shortest amount of time.** The result of this radio show broadcast, and the power of using Twitter as a focus group or resource room is evident on the following pages. *We thank all who contributed, and have listed them next to link shared. Special thanks to @SharonMcP Sharon McPherson who helped organize this list with us for you to have one organized list to shorten the investigation process.*

139

Desktop Twitter Applications

Twhirl - http://twhirl.org

A pc desktop app that lets you track and update tweets without having a browser window open.

Contributed by @WarrenWhitlock

Twitterific - http://iconfactory.com/software/twitterrific

A desktop Twitter client for Macs only.

Contributed by @SorterSuzy

MadTwitter - http://www.madtwitter.com

A Windows app that's inspired by the Mac application, Twitterrific.

Contributed by @MarkRess

Tweetdeck - http://www.tweetdeck.com

Adobe Air desktop application that enables users to split tweets into topic or group specific columns. Contributed by @CoachDeb

Pwytter - http://www.pwytter.com

Twitter client for Windows, Mac & Linux. Available in 14 languages.

Contributed by @SharonMcP

Twitux - http://fosswire.com/2008/03/31/twitux-a-gnome-twitter-client

A native GTK/Gnome desktop client for Twitter.

Contributed by @SharonMcP

Mobile Twitter Applications

Twinkle - http://tapulous.com/twinkle

A Twitter application for the iPhone.

Twitter for iPhone - http://twitterforiphone.com

Update your status, follow your friends, view profiles and add new friends from your iPhone. Contributed by @SharonMcP

Ping.fm - http://ping.fm

Use AIM, GTalk, iGoogle, WAP, iPhone/iPod Touch, SMS or E-mail and let Ping.fm relay your message to a multitude of social networking sites, including Twitter. Contributed by @Blogi360

Tiny Twitter - http://tinytwitter.com

Love tweeting from your mobile device but don't want to get dinged for updates and double dinged for friend's updates arriving via SMS? Tiny Twitter is just what you are looking for!

Contributed by @SharonMcP

TwitterBerry - http://orangatame.com/products/twitterberry

A mobile client for posting updates to Twitter from your Blackberry. Contributed by @SharonMcP

PocketTweets - http://www.pockettweets.com

Update your Twitter status from anywhere using your iPhone.

Contributed by @SharonMcP

Twitter File Sharing Applications

Twitpic - http://twitpic.com

Enables you to share photos on Twitter and let your followers comment on them. Contributed by @Shane

Tweetr - http://www.tweet-r.com

Desktop application that enables you to send files to your followers and take pictures using your webcam. Contributed by @SharonMcP

Tweetcube - http://tweetcube.com

A file sharing service for Twitter. You can upload as many images, archives, videos and songs as you want and share them on Twitter with your followers. Contributed by @SharonMcP

Twixxer - http://twixxer.com

A photo and video sharing component for Twitter. It is comprised of a browser add-on and a web service that enables you to view videos and picturesdirectly from your Twitter home page.

Contributed by @SharonMcP

Send Video and Voice Twitter Updates

Jott - http://jott.com

Jott.com's voice-to-text service converts your spoken words into Tweets - all with a simple phone call..

Contributed by @DaveTaylor

TwitSay - http://twitsay.com

Enables you to make a voice "tweet" from your phone that will then be added to your Twitter timeline. Contributed by @SharonMcP

Utterz - http://www.utterz.com

Utters can be audio, video, pictures and text. You can create or join a discussion from any mobile phone or computer.

Contributed by @WarrenWhitlock

Phweet - http://phweet.com

Lets you accept calls with one click from your Twitter page or Twitter clients. You don't need to download or share anything more to talk because the call is contained within a PhweetUrl; a smart link that calls you. Contributed by @SharonMcP

TwitterFone - http://www.twitterfone.com

A free service that lets you update your Twitter feed using your voice from any mobile or cell phone. You call it, speak your tweet, and hang up. A short while later, your tweet will be posted on Twitter.

Contributed by @WayneSutton

Seesmic - http://www.seesmic.com

Seesmic is a video sharing service just like YouTube, Vimeo, Viddler, etc. However; when you post a video on Seesmic, it can send an update to your Twitter account. Contributed by @Blogi360

Eyejot This! - http://www.eyejot.com

A bookmarklet that enables you to send Eyejot video messages pertaining to web sites you visit directly to your Twitter account. Your Eyejot message will automatically contain a link to the page you're on along with the page title. You create your Eyejot video using only your webcam and microphone. Contributed by @SharonMcP

Research, Find and Manage Followers

Twitter Search - http://search.twitter.com

Enables you to find out what's happening in the world beyond your personal Twitter timeline. Twitter Search (formerly Summize) helps you filter all the real-time information coursing through Twitter.

Contributed by @AdamDesAutels and @WarrenWhitlock

Twitterholic - http://www.twitterholic.com

Shows the top 100 users on Twitter based on number of followers.

Contributed by @MarkRess

Top 100 Tweeters - http://www.twittercounter.com/100.php

The top 100 most popular Twitter users. Updated daily.

Contributed by @GeekMommy

TwitDir - http://www.twitdir.com

A Twitter User Directory. Contributed by @Blogi360

Tweetbeep - http://tweetbeep.com

Like Google alerts for Twitter! Sends alerts by email when a tweet matches your search. Contributed by @RoyMontero & @MariSmith

Twemes - http://twemes.com

Through the use of twemes or hashtags (#) you can view what people are talking about across the Twitterverse. Contributed by @AdamDesAutels and @WarrenWhitlock

Tweetscan - http://www.tweetscan.com

A real-time search engine for Twitter that will also deliver results via email. ontributed by @CoachDeb

Twist - http://twist.flaptor.com

Enables you to see and graphically chart popular trends being discussed on Twitter. Contributed by @SuzysPlace

Tweet 2 Tweet - http://tweet2tweet.com

Tracks the public timelines to collect data in order to view conversations between two Twitter users. Contributed by @LindaLocke

TwitterSafe - http://twittersafe.com

If you lost your Followers, Following, and Replies on 'Black Tweetsday', you know the panic and fear that raced through the Twitterverse. Now there is a solution, to keep YOU Safe..TwitterSafe! Your One-Click Backup and Restoration Vault! Contributed by @CoachDeb

Tweetake - http://tweetake.com

Lets you back up your followers, friends, tweets and everything else that you may have on Twitter. Contributed by @CoachDeb

TweetStats - http://tweetstats.com

Provides colourful graphs on month-to-month, daily and hourly tweets, people replied to most, and interfaces preferred for individual Twitter users. Contributed by @MattSurfs

TwitterBuzz - http://www.twitterbuzz.com

TwitterBuzz collects links that are mentioned on Twitter and arranges them in order of popularity. You can view links mentioned in the last hour, day, week, or forever (since archival started). Contributed by @MarkRess

Twitter Karma - http://dossy.org/twitter/karma

A flash application that fetches your friends and followers from Twitter when you click the "Whack!" button, then displays them for you, letting you quickly paginate through them.

Contributed by @DaveWebb

Twitscoop - http://www.twitscoop.com

Twitscoop crawls hundreds of tweets every minute and extracts the words which are mentionned more often than usual. The result is displayed in a Tag Cloud, using the following rule: the hotter the subject, the bigger the tag text. Contributed by @SharonMcP

Quotably - http://quotably.com

In addition to seeing what's the most popular conversations on Twitter, Quotably.com also enables you to read the entire conversations of Twitter users. Contributed by @SharonMcP

DoesFollow - http://doesfollow.com

Answers the question "does (Twitter username) follow (Twitter username)?" Contributed by @SharonMcP

Twellow - http://www.twellow.com

Enables you to search for people on Twitter or, if you don't exactly know who you're looking for, you can search by categories sorted by keywords related to such things as industry, interests, or hobbies. Patty said this about Twellow on the TwitterHandbook blog, *"I think this will be a great resource for all Twitter users to find people on Twitter they have something in common with based on niche."*

Contributed by @littlebytesnews

My Tweeple - http://www.mytweeple.com

Lists people you are following and your Twitter followers in alphabetic order. You can follow, unfollow, block or ding spammers. Ding=bad. Contributed by @SharonMcP

Twitterdex - http://twitterdex.com

Publicize your Twitter account as well as find other popular Twitterers.

Contributed by @SharonMcP

TwitterLocal - http://www.twitterlocal.net

Lets you find Twitter users around a certain area. Just enter a city, state, postal code, choose the range of miles you want to include and hit the button. Contributed by @SharonMcP

TwitterPoster - http://twitterposter.com

Provides a visual representation of the degree of influence of the Twitter users. Contributed by @SharonMcP

PicoBuzz - Your Buzz Chart for Twitter - http://www.picobuzz.com

A web app that extracts current buzzlike activity from Twitter. Data is pulled–and statistics are updated–frequently (on the order of minutes). Cool tool to see what the hottest trends of the moment are. Contributed by @SharonMcP

TwitterSnooze - http://twittersnooze.com

Lets you temporarily block the tweets of people that get noisy for a 24-hour period. This is especially good when someone goes to a conference that you're following and tweeting in blog-like fashion the day's events. Contributed by @SharonMcP

Locate and Publicize Twitter Meetups (Tweetups)

Triangle Tweetups - http://triangletweetup.pbwiki.com

Schedule of meetups of Twitter users from NC.

Contributed by @WayneSutton

Twitzu Events for Twitter - http://www.twitzu.com

Having a meetup, get together or party? Publicize it on Twitzu while blasting it out to your Twitter followers. Contributed by @SharonMcP

Browser and Blog Twitter Applications

Flock Social Media Web Browser - http://flock.com

Flock makes it easy to discover, access, create and share videos, photos, blogs, feeds and comments across social communities, including Twitter. Contributed by @flocker

TwitterCounter - http://www.twittercounter.com

A counter for bloggers and webmasters that shows the number of followers you have on Twitter. Contributed by @WarrenWhitlock

Twitzer - http://shorttext.com/twitzer.aspx

A Firefox extension that lets you post tweets longer than 140 characters.

Contributed by @SharonMcP

TwitterFox - https://addons.mozilla.org/en-US/firefox/addon/5081

A Firefox Addon which allows you to update and view your friends' status without logging into Twitter on the web. Contributed by @LisaPreston

RSS2Twitter - http://www.pivari.com/rss2twitter.html

A freeware perl tool (or a Windows executable) to send to Twitter (batch) the links and posts of a RSS feed. Contributed by @MarkRess

Shareaholic - http://shareaholic.com   Makes it easy for you to submit the web page you're on to your favorite social, sharing and bookmarking services. Contributed by @MarkRess

TwittyTunes - http://www.foxytunes.com/twittytunes

A FoxyTunes companion Firefox extension that allows you to post your currently playing songs to Twitter with a click. Contributed by @MarkRess

TweetMyBlog - http://www.tweetmyblog.com

Twitter Plugin for Wordpress that automatically posts to Twitter when you update your blog. Contributed by @SharonMcP

TwitterCard - http://twittercard.com

A Twitter blog widget that acts as your Twitter business card by showing your recent status, picture and location. Contributed by @SharonMcP

Twitterdoodle - http://www.lessnau.com/twitterdoodle

Wordpress plugin that creates automatic mashup posts relevant to your site's content from the daily chatter that goes on at Twitter. Contributed by @SharonMcP

Twitter Badge - http://www.widgetbox.com/widget/twitter

A Twitter widget you can add to your blog or website to keep your readers up-to-date on your latest tweets. Contributed by @SharonMcP

Feedtweeter - http://feedtweeter.com

Feedtweeter adds your Plurks and Identi.ca updates to Twitter and the other way aound in a sane way, but it (should) work with any RSS feed. Contributed by @SharonMcP

TwitThis - http://www.twitthis.com

When visitors to your website click on the TwitThis button or link, it takes the URL of the webpage and creates a shorter URL using TinyURL. Then visitors can send this shortened URL and a description of the webpage to all of their friends on Twitter. You can also add the TwitThis bookmarklet to your browser's toolbar to send a message through Twitter about any page you are viewing. Contributed by @SharonMcP

TwitBin - http://www.twitbin.com

Send and receive Twitter updates, right from your Firefox browser.

Contributed by @SharonMcP

TwitterBook - https://addons.mozilla.org/en-US/firefox/addon/6966

Firefox add-on that enables you to Tweet your favorite sites when you bookmark them on your browser. Contributed by @SharonMcP

TwitterBar - https://addons.mozilla.org/en-US/firefox/addon/4664 TwitterBar allows you to post to Twitter from Firefox's address bar. Contributed by @SharonMcP

Chirrup - http://chirrup.angryamoeba.co.uk

A Twitter comment system for your blog. Contributed by @SharonMcP

Twitterfeed - http://twitterfeed.com

Checks your blog's feed at the intervals you specify and post any new items to your Twitter followers. Contributed by @SharonMcP

Web-Based Twitter Resources

Twitrefresh - http://www.twitrefresh.com

A web-based application that automatically refreshes your Twitter homepage every 60 seconds. Contributed by @SharonMcP

Tweetlater - http://www.tweetlater.com

Enables you to schedule future-dated tweets, automatically follow new users and send automated thank you notes to your new followers. Contributed by @SuzysPlace

Alt Code Characters - http://www.alt-codes.net

Enables you to add symbols such as hearts, smiley faces, the sun, musical notes and more to your Tweets using the alt key and 0-255 decimal numbers. Contributed by @MariSmith

Twiddict - http://twiddict.com/login Lets you tweet even when Twitter is down. Tweet your heart out through Twiddict and avoid life-changing withdrawal symptoms during Twitter downtime. Contributed by @CoachDeb

Twiffid - http://www.twiffid.com

Automatically detects the feeds of the websites your Twitter friends have listed in their Twitter profiles and presents them to you in a Twitter-like format. Contributed by @JPmicek

OutTwit – http://OutTwit.com

An add-in for Outlook. Andrea Kalli commented on the Twitter Handbook blog, "I'm in Outlook all day and it just makes it easier for me to browse, post, and reply to Twitter posts."

Contributed by Andrea Kalli

TwitterMail - http://www.twittermail.com

Enables you to send Twiter updates from your email client. Will also send you an email of all @ replies sent to you. Contributed by @SharonMcP

Twitter Ratio - http://twitterratio.com/Default.aspx

Your Twitter Ratio is the ratio of your followers to friends (or people who you follow). It is measured with the TFF Ratio (Twitter Follower-Friend Ratio). The higher the ratio, the more Twitter heat you pack. Contributed by @Corvida

ReplyBot - http://www.financialaidpodcast.com/replybot

Scans the last 20 replies in your stream and auto-follows everyone who has replied to you recently. Contributed by @SharonMcP

Twitturly - http://twitturly.com

Twitt(url)y is a service for tracking what URLs people are discussing on Twitter. Kind of like Digg for Twitter. Contributed by @SaleZy

Twittervision - http://twittervision.com

See tweets from all over the world on an interactive map.

Contributed by @MarkRess

Twordy - http://twordy.com

Twordy lets you post as many characters as you wish. The service simply updates your Twitter account with a link to the longer, wordier, Twordy. Contributed by @SharonMcP

Tweetburner - http://tweetburner.com

Tweetburner lets you track what happens with the links you share on Twitter. Contributed by @SharonMcP

Tweetmarks - http://tweetmarks.com

Easily organize the links you share on Twitter! Tweetmarks can even add your links to del.icio.us automatically! Contributed by @SharonMcP

TweetAnswers - http://tweetanswers.com

Like merging Yahoo! Answers with Twitter. Contributed by @SharonMcP

SecretTweet - http://secrettweet.com

Tweet your secrets to the Twitterverse anonymously. Shhhh!

Contributed by @SharonMcP

TweetUpsideDown - http://brad.globeproductions.com.au/twitter_side_down

A fun app created by @4fthawaiian that enables you to send upside down tweets. (*This is just for kicks and to get your readers to think differently by reading your tweets differently. Well, at least that's my take on this fun app. @CoachDeb*)

Tweetclouds - http://www.tweetclouds.com

Make a word cloud from a public Twitter stream.

Contributed by @JPmicek

Twitscoop - http://www.twitscoop.com

Twitscoop was built to help you stay on top of twitter's hot topics or discussions. Contributed by @JPmicek

Here's where you'll realize how the answer to the question, "What are you doing?" can have very different answers, from "I'm watching history take place at the Olympics", to "Did you just feel an Earthquake?"

Through an automated algorithm, twitscoop crawls hundreds of tweets every minute and extracts the words which are mentioned more often than usual. The result is displayed in a Tag Cloud, using the following rule: the hotter, the bigger (no joke).

As a result, twitscoop and tracking services like it, enables you to stay on top of things in a matter of seconds, often way before mainstream media has a chance to cover it.

This is the social media revolution that will change the way people send and receive communication about what's happening around the world.

PimpMyNews http://PimpMyNews.com is a very cool service that literally makes your blog talk!

This is fantastic for the visually impaired who need their tweets to talk to them and stay connected.

It's also great if you'd like to shut your eyes, relax a bit and listen to tweets or blogs.

Worth checking into.

Very cool.

Did we miss one of your favorite apps? Do you have an update to one of these apps that the Twitterverse needs to know about? Add your contributions to this chapter at:

http://TwitterHandbook.com/blog/apps

Subscribers to the Online Twitter Handbook http://TwitterHandbook.com will get regular updates on popular Twitter apps, changes and the latest, coolest apps coming out that support Twitter and other social media networks.

NOTE:

We've done our best in compiling and organizing the most popular Twitter Apps being used by Tweeters. However, some of these apps may change, or no longer be supported by the time this book goes to print. Please post a comment on our blog post above if you notice one of the previous apps are obsolete so we can revise our list. Thanks!

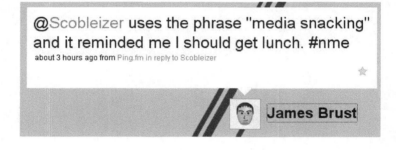

Chapter 11

Glossary of terms for Twitter

Twixicon of Tweetspeak and Frequently Used Abbreviations

Special thanks to tweeter who helped Compile Twitter Glossary for the Twitter Handbook: Dr. Todd Fiegel Follow him on Twitter @DrTodd

If you've been on Twitter for any length of time, you've noticed there's a lingo used that seems like only insiders know.

Well now, you're an insider and can learn all the fun, tribal lingo used on Twitter and can tweet to impress your friends.

If you have a word to add to this list, please do so by placing a comment on the online version of this book at:

http://TwitterHandbook.com/blog/glossary

Twitter Glossary & More

@	a) reply b) when you're speaking to someone, used in front of their username
dm	direct message (when speaking to someone privately on Twitter)
drive-by tweet	single interruptive tweet - the tweep doesn't stay for conversation - they just tweet & run
fweeps	Twitter friends = comprised of Friends + People (or peeps) = fweeps (see also peeps, tweeple, tweeps)
halftwit	tweeter who doesn't quite "get it" (see also nittwit)
mistweet	a) misspoken tweet, b) tweet mistakenly sent as reply instead of DM (direct message) DOH!
nittwit	tweeter who doesn't quite "get it" (see also half-twit)
peeps	a) slang for People b) your entourage on Twitter c) Twitter followers or users (see also fweeps, tweeple, tweeps)
pretwext	a misleading or disguised intention of a tweeter
shoutout	recognition of another through special mention in one's tweet (giving "props")
t-;)	Twitter wink, twink
timeline	display of successive tweets of your own, your friends, replies to you, or everybody on Twitter
TUI	tweeting under the influence, aka drunk-tweeting (see also twipsy)
twaddict	one who is addicted to Twitter and must be connected to Twitter and needs Twitter to LIVE!

Glossary of Terms for Twitter

twaddiction	the state of having to be connected to Twitter in order to talk to your friends... sitting across the table
twaiting	tweeting while waiting
Twamu	name of whale that appears when Twitter is overloaded (see also tweizure)
twater	tweet you later
TWD	tweeting while driving (tisk tisk tisk)
tweeple	a) People who tweet b) Twitter users (see also fweeps, peeps, tweeps)
tweeps	a) Peeps who tweet b) Twitter users (see also fweeps, tweeple, tweeps)
tweetworthy	being worthy of a tweetback
tweetable	being worthy of a tweetback
tweetaholic	one who must tweet (see also twaddict, twitaholic)
tweetaholism	the state of needing to tweet, get tweet, and be connected to Twitter (see also twaddiction)
tweetard	one who is Twitter-deficient (troll)
tweetback	tweet reply @ username in question
tweeterboxes	those who tweet excessively about mundane things
tweeter	one who tweets (a person using Twitter to speak to hundreds of friends/contacts at once)
tweetheart	tweeter with a special connection to another
tweetin	gathering of tweeters to meet and tweet (see also tweetup)
tweetup	gathering of tweeters to meet and tweet or not to tweet either way they meet up in person (see also tweetin)
twegotist	one who believes his own tweets are of paramount importance

tweizure	when Twitter overloads and Twamu the whale appears (see also Twamu)
tweetspeak	language and terms used by and unique to tweeters (see also twitspeak, twictionary, twixicon)
tweetstream	combination of incoming and outgoing tweets of one user or one topic of conversation among tweeters (also twitstream)
twempo	frequency of one's tweets
twetiquette	rules of courtesy concerning tweeting
twexpert	one who is highly regarded for knowledge about Twitter and tweeting or texting
twexting	tweeting through texting via phone or similar device
twextaddict	one whose gotta have text
twextually active	one who tweets, texts, or gets text - often
twibute	accord or honor given to one tweeter by another
twiccup	unexpected loss of tweets or friends/followers by Twitter, often seen as symptom of tweizure
twickle	state of delight experienced by another's tweet
twickster	tweeter who misleads another, usually in a joking way
twictionary	compilation of terms used by and applied to tweeters (see also twixicon, tweetspeak, twitspeak)
twID	tweeter's handle ("@" name) aka: username on Twitter
twidbit	a morsel of information within a tweet
twidcrumbs	reverse succession of tweets, following a topic backwards to its origin
twidget	tiny Twitter badge containing recent tweets, placed on blog or website

Glossary of Terms for Twitter

twidjit	term, often of endearment, for one not yet well-versed in tweeting (see also twincompoop)
twidnap	finding tweeps to follow by studying list of another's list or Search.Twitter stream
twignoramus	tweeter who ignores common twetiquette
twimbuktu	arrival point of tweets that mysteriously disappear (see twiccup)
twimid	reluctant to tweet or enter conversation
twincompoop	term, often of endearment, for one not yet well-versed in tweeting (see also twidjit)
twingling	pleasant sensation experienced when tweeting
twink	emoticon t-;), a Twitter wink
twip	a brief, often humorous, interjection or response
twipsy	tweeting while slightly inebriated, often leading to TUI (see also TUI)
twirgin	one who has not yet tweeted
twis (dis)	a tweeted dis-regard or dis-dain) of someone
twinterview	interview conducted in 140-character chunks or 140 seconds
twitaholic	one who loves Twitter so much that they can't leave home without it (see also twaddict, tweetaholic)
twitarrhea	a) state of overtweeting by one user; b) Twitter's release of all tweets stored during technical issues (see also twitstipation)
twitcrastinate	putting off other activities or obligations in order to tweet
twitillate	to provoke or arouse thought while tweeting
twitorial	step-by-step guide to tweeting

twitpitch	sales pitch on Twitter
twitspeak	language and terms used by and unique to tweeters (see also tweetspeak, twictionary, twixicon)
twitstipation	lack of free-flowing tweets when Twitter has technical issues (see also twitarrhea)
twitstream	combination of incoming and outgoing tweets of one user or one topic of conversation among tweeters (also tweetstream)
twitterectomy	ridding oneself of Twitter use and deleting your account
twitterati	glamorous tweeter A-list followed by many)
twitterexia	refusal to eat because of desire to tweet
twittermentia	tendency to forget one's previous tweets
twitterpated	particularly smitten with Twitter and tweeting
twitterverse	the Twitter world (The Twitter Universe)
twittip	a tweeted tip on a specific topic, Twitter tip (also: Twip)
twittish	erratic behavior by a tweeter
twivyeur	one who watches others tweet but does not participate
twixicism	a witty tweet
twixicon	compilation of terms used by and applied to tweeters (see also tweetspeak, twictionary, twitspeak)
twixotic	state of tweeting oddly or curiously
twypo	a mistyped word or character on Twitter in order 2 fit tweet in 140 characters

Glossary of Terms for Twitter

"how to say more with less"

2	to, too, two
4	for, four
2mrw	tomorrow
2nite	tonight
b	be
b4	before
bbialw	be back in a little while
bbl	be back later
bc	because
brb	be right back
btw	by the way
c	see
cya	see ya
fav, fave	favorite
imho	in my humble opinion
imo	in my opinion
l8, l8r	late, later (8 may substitute for this syllable in many words)
lite	light
lmfao	laughin my frickin ass off
lmao	laughing my ass off
lol	laughing out loud (common) but also lots of love
nite	night

np	no problem
omg	oh my gosh, oh my God, oh my goodness
pls, plz	please
rotf	rolling on the floor
rotflmao	rolling on the floor laughing my ass off
rotflmaoiapmp	rolling on the floor laughing my ass off I almost pee'd my pants!
thx, ty, TX	Thanks, thank you, Thanks a lot
ttfn	ta-ta for now
ttyl	talk to you later
u	you
u r	you are
ur	your, you're, you are
w, w/	with
wth	what the heck, what the hell (other final consonants may also be used)
y	why
yw	you're welcome

Chapter 12

Speed vs. Spelling

Does spelling & grammar count for anything on Twitter?

In the Twitterverse this would read:

Does spelin count 4 anythin on Twitter?

If that sentence bugs you because there's an "L" missing in spelling and a "g" missing from anything, I have just 3 words 4 U:

Get over it!

On Twitter, in order to fit your thought in one tweet, you often need to be creative. Very creative.

Complete sentences are not required like your English teacher taught you. Double letters in words become irrelevant. And using numbers in the place of words is a gr8 way 4 u 2 squeeze more into less space.

Now, if you're a stickler (or as we refer to different communication styles in our book "Secrets of Online Persuasion", we say, if you're a "Bishop" or a High "C" Compliant type) then spelling and grammar will matter... TO YOU. But not to the rest of the Twitterverse.

167

Stop shaking your head!

Actually, no – don't take my word for it. Instead, ask the Twitterverse what THEY think. Then tweet accordingly.

You may think spelling and grammar are of utmost importance when communicating anything over the Web.

You may be right. But Twitter style communication is all about getting your point across in 140 characters or less – and doing it quickly.

This hangup on spelling may become a huge inhibitor for you if you focus on proper ways to craft a sentence, instead of what Twitter is designed to do – deliver FAST communication in succinct format.

Here's where you need to evaluate in order to determine your style of tweeting. Examine who your choice clientele is in order to determine if you'll always use proper spelling or if you'll take allowances here and there.

Make a list by answering the following questions to get you started:

Who is your ideal client?

Is she a stickler for details?

Is he in the post-baby boomer generation? (aka: post 60 years old?)

Are they accountants, attorneys or English teachers?

If any of the above comprise the majority of your clientele, then I'm afraid you'll have to stick to real words and simply use two or three tweets to get your point across instead of trying to squeeze everything into one tweet.

It does take some time to cleverly eliminate unnecessary words from your tweets. In fact, I wish my English teacher assigned this to me in college, because I was a verbose writer back then! But the more I tweet, the more I realize how verbose my communication is, and how easily I can eliminate words and yet make a point – and do it more concisely.

Internet marketing tip in regards to SEO (Search Engine Optimization) when using Twitter:

The one time you do not want to use shortcuts in your tweets is for your keywords for your business / niche / industry.

That's because Twitter is highly searchable and extremely effective for SEO. So in order to take advantage of that benefit and get yourself listed on the front page of Google's search – be sure to always spell your keywords properly.

More on SEO and optimizing your tweets in future chapters. We're still covering the basics of Twitter. (Or have we already moved into advanced territory?)

To show you how it works on Twitter, let me give

(See glossary for examples of abbreviated words used on Twitter and in online chat rooms to expedite your message.)

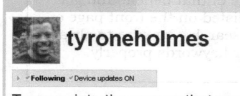

tyroneholmes

Following   Device updates ON

To grow into the person that you want to be.
You must first plant, cultivate and then only
then can you harvest.

half a minute ago from web

Chapter 13

21 Tips to Terminating Twitter Trolls

If you're reading this chapter because you've been visited by a twitter troll or been brand-jacked, CONGRATULATIONS!!! This is the sign that you've succeeded in brand recognition and are generating enough buzz and success in order to be visited by the haters whose only mission in life is to take happy and successful people down.

Sadly, these types of people have not gotten the positive attention they desperately crave. They attempt to get negative attention because they've learned that negative attention is better than no attention.

I spent the first decade of my career as a behavioral analyst and social worker where I received extensive training in conflict resolution—many times training was through hands-on experience.

Ultimately, if someone hasn't figured out how to develop healthy friendships and business relationships, they resort to the belief that they will always be unsuccessful, and therefore not care if their actions online (which remain a permanent record) reflect poorly on their reputation—because they typically don't have a reputation to lose.

Another aspect of those who attempt to brand-jack your successful brand in an attempt to try and make you look bad (when it merely has a boomerang effect and makes them look bad) is that it gives them purpose to their day.

In the blogosphere these types of people are called "trolls". Unfortunately, trolls are not successful enough to be busy with contract work of their own, so with all this extra time on their hands, they seek out those who have too much work and activity online in the faulty hopes that they'll sabotage their business and get the fall-out. This never happens because any successful professional can see through the troll's actions for what it really is – a poor attempt at getting some sort of attention. Successful people know the difference and can easily realize who the truly successful people are online.

The best word to describe the emotional nature of this type of individual is the German word **shadenfreude**. This is the pleasure one gets from watching someone else suffer. It's their only hope of a momentary feeling of pleasure because for a moment, they felt they were better than you. For a moment. When that feeling goes away, they tweet you again with some form of negative tweets.

Your true fans, followers, and clients know what's going on when they see someone continually stalk you just to get in your Twitter stream. Trust your followers to recognize the silliness for what it is. You can count on your follower's increased loyalty during this time and in fact it actually serves to strengthen your bond with them in a way that only comes when facing a crisis. It only makes the troll look bad and you look more successful for being the target of a troll.

A nice side benefit to being targeted by the trolls is that your clients and followers actually grow MORE supportive of you and rally to your defense. Some think trolls serve a useful purpose for just this reason! Some tweeters have actively tried to attract a troll to give them link love. (This is the love you get from search engines from the links sent to your Twitter username with any @ reply you receive.)

Nothing like creating a huge tribe of raving fans that give you link love! The more they @ your name, the more they're sending YOU links, and increasing the number of times people are @-ing you, which increases your influence rank—not the trolls. So in effect, their actions are resulting in the exact opposite of what they desire for you. You may consider thanking them – at least with a smile every time they visit your stream.

So, how do you handle all this type of attention when you attract enough followers to begin gaining the attention of the trolls online?

We'll share the 21 tips our friend Mari Smith penned after dealing with someone who was jealous of her success and had too much time on his hands. Mari has been dubbed "the Pied Piper of Facebook" by Fast Company. She is a Facebook Business Coach who recently attracted some troll who was jealous of her success with the thousands of followers she had on Facebook.

The good thing for Mari is that she had a team of people who had dealt with this issue themselves and were able to encourage her, lift her up, and share tips on how to deal with this type of behavior. Below are the tips she compiled from all the wonderful supporters who know, love, and trust her as the consummate professional that she is.

Special thanks go to someone you should follow @MariSmith and thank her for sharing her learning lessons with you in this book below on how to terminate the trolls who've recognized your success and don't like it. Use her tips when you first notice a public tweet @ you from your stalker (troll/abuser).

Mari's 21 Tips:

1. Don't panic. Try to understand the person may have psychological issues and simply want attention, and is not getting enough on their own merits.

2. Go to the troll's Twitter account and make sure you BLOCK them immediately. Go to the person's actual Twitter page http://twitter.com/trollnamehere and look under the avatar montage of the people they follow and you'll see a link that says "block trollnamehere"— click the link that says "Block."

    A window will pop up confirming you want to block them. Click the button choice that says: "Okay I still want to block this person."

3. Do NOT tweet the troll's @ name publicly. This only brings them visibility, back links, and the attention they want from you. The more you tweet their name/Twitter ID, the more you'll encourage them to continue.

4. Do not tweet out to your followers to block your stalker's @ name for the reasons described in #3 above. Instead, send periodic tweets when necessary such as:

    "I only ever tweet from 1 account: @marismith All others are fakes. Plz block/ignore the trolls. Thx."

5. Take legal action immediately. Capture screen shots. Save them all in a folder. Contact your attorney/speak with your legal department immediately. Have them create a Cease and Desist (C&D) notice and send it to the troll/abuser/brand-jacker.

    (This step will depend on the severity of the abuse. But it must always be taken into consideration when they attempt to illegally use your trademarked brand. I sent a C&D to my abuser and basically received an "eff you" note back. LOL!)

Let your attorney do the work. And if your attorney can't reach the abuser, use Google, Facebook, and other searches to find their address and contact information.

6. Reach out for help in private (by Twitter DM, for example) from people in your community more experienced on Twitter and/or handling abusers than you may be.

7. Be vigilant about searching for our own name on http://search.twitter.com as @yourname, yourname, and your name. Also search for your name and your stalkers' name to catch any bad tweets. (See Step 10 for what to do next).
(See note below re: reputation management.)

8. Search for your domain name or other key terms the troll keeps tweeting. And/or set up http://tweetbeep.com for key names, words, and phrases (Tweetbeep works like http://GoogleAlerts.com which you should already be using to track your name, company name and products online).

9. Search for your stalker's name in various formats to track conversations they may be having about you with others. When appropriate, follow those other people and interject when necessary by following them, then sending them a DM (direct message)—see Step 10. [NOTE: You can only send DMs to people who follow you back].

10. If your stalker has set up a fake account(s), search for that account—especially @ replies to them.

    a. Follow tweeps who are following the fake account.

    b. Follow tweeps who've sent @ replies to the fake account. When they follow you back, you can DM them and let them know you're the real @MariSmith (replace with your name there).

c. If they don't follow you back, send them an @ tweet in the public timeline simply asking them to follow you back, or letting them know you only have one account and this is it. If you have other means of contacting that person such as Facebook, email, etc. use that instead so they know they're following an illegitimate account.

11. Send DM's to alert those unaware that they are tweeting to a fake account or a Twitter abuser stalking you. Suggested tweet:

> "Plz note U R tweeting 2 FAKE acct by troll stalking me. BLOCK @fakename & @abusername. Thx."

12. Report the abuser to Twitter. Go to http://help.twitter.com and search for keywords such as abuse, fake, troll, harass, harassment, twitter-jack, brand-jack depending on your situation. Results may take you to the thread on GetStatisfaction.com. (See next tip.)

13. Search http://getsatisfaction.com for a report similar to your case. If you don't find one, add your own. Twitter's team reads GetSatisfaction.

14. Watch the troll's twitter account for patterns in their online activity.

15. Vary your own activity. If you're normally active in the afternoons, switch to early mornings.

16. Do your absolute best to not let the abuser get to you. Muster all your effort and ignore them. Remember, this is all a part of being mega successful. Trolls don't bother tweeters who don't have any influence. So count it as a compliment.

17. Be persistent. You have every right to continue your user experience on Twitter unmarred by trolls abusing you online. Several friends had advised me to lay off Twitter for a stretch of time. I was so reluctant to take the advice; I didn't want to sacrifice my continuity in my connection with my peeps. So instead, I stepped up my activity more and rallied even more support.

18. Remind yourself any publicity is good publicity. Though it may be a temporarily unpleasant experience, you're actually raising your own visibility and getting links back to your Twitter account and websites.

19. Be positive, polite, and patient. Professionals always handle adversity professionally.

20. Remember that those who know, like, and trust YOU and recognize and admire YOUR BRAND will simply ignore the adverse activity and rally to support you. One negative troll on Twitter cannot take down what you've built.

   Also, keep in mind it can actually be a *compliment* that you have become so successful, so visible that a troll (most likely jealous) has deemed you worthy of bugging. I know, it's a tough reframe, but you may need to develop a thicker skin as you grow your business.

21. Do your best to look for a silver lining, a positive reframe. Often events in life happen for a reason. There may be a powerful lesson for you to get. You might look for how your experience and the way you respond may benefit others such as I've done here.

NOTE: This is referred to as "reputation management" and monitoring your brand online is something you should be doing anyway in order to track what people are saying about your products/services/books/etc. both positive or negative, in order to jump in and respond.

A great way to do get notified anytime someone mentions your name or company online is by using Google Alerts. http://www.googlealerts.com

It's currently a free service, and you should not wait to be targeted by someone suffering from shadenfreude to be diligent in tracking your brand online.

Have your reputation management VA (virtual assistant) or legal department be in charge of all this so you can focus on what you do best—helping other people!

One last thing to keep in mind as Twitter grows in popularity and attracts all types of people to a free service.

Don't take any negative tweets about someone else at face value. Do your own research. Google people's names to see what real professionals are saying about the people you are looking to do business with.

Gossip is just as much of a problem online as it is in "the real world".

Our philosophy is to not engage in negative tweeting or gossip – ever – because it doesn't do anything to produce business results. And that's what you're there for.

Let your character shine through, and your real fans and clients will see the obvious difference between you and your trolls.

> Great minds discuss ideas. Average minds discuss events. Small minds discuss people.
> by Eleanor Roosevelt
> 08:11 PM August 22, 2008 from web
>
> ☆
>
> **Andrew Kelly**
> Tweet!

PART THREE

*Influence & Persuasion Strategies
to Position & Brand Yourself on
Twitter & Other Social Networks*

Chapter 14

How is Twitter Different from Traditional Marketing?

Keep in mind Twitter is simply the tool for easy micro-blogging. There are other services similar to Twitter, but it just so happens that right now anybody who's anybody is on Twitter.

In fact, a song just came out to that effect. "You're No One If You're Not On Twitter" by JB Walker from http://www.ihatemornings.com (You can watch his video at: http://TwitterHandbook.com/blog/videos and laugh with us if you can relate.)

As long as the party is on Twitter, more will come. But anywhere we talk about Twitter, we could just as easily be talking about other mico-blogging services like Plurk, Identi.ca, Jaiku, Pownce or OpenMicroBlogging.com.

Whether Twitter sells its tool to the highest bidder and operates under a new name in the near future, or we all take our party to a different micro-blogging service provider, all the early-adopters who were part of the Twitter Revolution will always be "tweeting" in one form or another.

Since Twitter is the most popular and active micro-blogging service around the world, we'll be using Twitter as the service of choice for this book. Just keep in mind, you can easily interchange "micro-blog" anytime Twitter is referenced.

It's not about the tool. It's about the communication revolution that's happening as we speak, tweet, and sleep.

Join in, or be left behind.

How is Twitter different from other marketing activities?

Who can get this message to Donald Trump for me? Can you please tell The Donald, "It's business. And it's *ALWAYS* personal."

With Twitter, you need to think 180 degrees differently from everything you've ever learned about traditional marketing. Your new model is: ***business is always personal.***

Women have been responsible for much of the social marketing that began a decade ago, when "social media" wasn't a hot buzz word.

Years before internet marketers knew about this tribe of social networkers, forums and online business chat rooms, there were thousands of work-at-home moms (WAHMs) who wanted to connect with other women who were in the same situation. Men who worked at home also joined in; there were online business forums as well as women-only focused organizations designed for the sole purpose of connecting one another to share resources, brainstorm ideas, and do business with one another.

Internet marketers came once they realized, "This is where our market is. They're hanging out at Ryze, Ecademy, and all of these other social networking places." Then there was MySpace, Facebook, Jaiku, Pownce, and now Twitter.

For stay-at-home moms, working moms, or home-based business owners, these networks gave them the ability to connect with one another when they were feeling isolated or disconnected from the rest of the business world who were forced to commute to work in a stuffy office building.

One phrase I'd hear over and over, when in-person conferences came around was, "I just can't get away. My husband doesn't want to be stuck for the weekend watching the kids while I run off to some conference."

Women felt handcuffed and shackled to their desks, because they couldn't participate in a lot of the live conferences. So, they did what women always do, they became resourceful and found another way. They started getting involved with teleconferences, forums, and all the different online places that gave them the ability to easily connect online – without having to travel anywhere.

When you hear the new buzz word "social media" all you need to know is that it's the same thing as Web 2.0 which was the big buzz word two to three years ago. I like to call it "new media marketing with lipstick on" because that's all social media really is.

The question on Twitter asks its members, "What are you doing?" Often, when businessmen see Twitter they think, "There's all of this social stuff. Whatever. Who cares about what you're doing? We have business to take care of. Sales to be made! Prospects to be converted! Let's get down to business."

But that's really not an accurate picture of how business deals have ever been done. Think about it.

On golf courses and in country clubs, people have always made personal connections that led to profitable business ventures of untold gains.

Getting to know a person's character, integrity and interests while on the golf course was one of the best "interviews" that could ever be conducted.

Business is always personal. And the more personal it gets, the more business gets done!

Twitter simply gives you the ability to get personal with people. The more personal you are, the better you'll connect with people who have similar interests, quirks, frustrations, and values as you.

There's something powerful about the tribe of people who share similar interests.

People will follow you just because you have the same name as them! But the best thing about Twitter is you can connect with people from around the world, regardless of their location. This expands your network immensely, and reduces the 6-degrees of separation very quickly.

Marketing on Twitter does not look anything like 'traditional marketing" where you give your prospects a sense of urgency by giving them a deadline to use a coupon. Rather it's much more subtle and inviting than that.

Don't come onto Twitter with the mindset, "It's all about business," or "Here's the product I'm launching." Unless you have a following that's used to that and wants that kind of notification, or unless you like rejection, that type of tweeting is not going to get you want you want.

Now there will be a time when it's okay to talk about the release of a new product you've been working on, especially if that's what your clients and followers expect from following you. Just don't **start** off with those types of tweets, or only deliver notification tweets of what you've got to sell. That's boring, and people will think you have no life. Not to mention, you will turn off the rest of the Twitterverse that's watching you, deciding whether you're follow-worthy or block-worthy.

You might have your own clients following and they may like knowing when you're doing a promotion for your latest product or service, but if you're trying to connect with people who aren't your clients yet, hold back on the sales pitch when you first join in the conversation. It is a turnoff. Provide value and give resources on Twitter.

INSIDER INFORMATION:

Women may never tweet this publicly, but they express sheer disgust with this type of in-your-face sales pitch when they're together. They can't stand when men come in to a social network and just try to pitch, pitch, pitch their products or services. Women are truly there to connect with one another. They are there to share resources and meet new friends. Many women feel isolated. Keep that in mind when you tweet. Think differently about your marketing strategy in an online social network, and you'll be moving in the right direction.

Both men and women solopreneurs love Twitter for the aspect that it brings people together. Hold the pitches off. Be personal. Share pictures instead of pitches. This is the place where it's okay to talk about your family and personal hobbies. It's almost expected.

Business owners who come on twitter and only talk about what they're doing in their work day are held in suspicion. We either think you lead a very boring life, or you're hiding something.

We live in a day of authenticity and radical transparency. There's no more hiding behind a "persona." People want to get to know YOU.

SHARE PICTURES ON TWITTER

www.TwitPic.com is a great tool for you to use from your phone, email account or the internet to share pictures with your followers.

It allows you to tweet pictures from the road and instantly share what you're doing. There is something that connects us when we are able to share in the experiences you are enjoying *right now.*

My friends and followers know me to be an avid book lover. The current book I'm reading at any given time comes with me wherever I go. (Yes, I'm a geek – so hush! Or go tweet that I'm a geek – I'm proud of it.)

What I didn't realize was how my book became this traveling mascot in whatever scene I shared from my iPhone as I would enjoy my weekends in Hawaii.

Whether I was in my backyard reading on the lanai with my boxer, Capitalista, seen here: http://twitpic.com/5z4u

Or whether the book came with me to the beach, as seen here: http://twitpic.com/6guw

My followers would look forward to where they'd find the book in the next picture link I tweeted directly from TwitPic.

Think creatively. Instead of just tweeting, this is the book I'm reading, snap a picture of it while you're in a setting you want to share with your followers. This is a great personal way to share a resource while simultaneously making a personal connection with them.

You can snap a picture and upload it to TwitPic via email or your mobile Web browser. You can send it directly from your iPhone, BlackBerry, or whatever phone you use that has access to email.

Within seconds of you sending the picture via email, it's online, ready for your followers to view and comment. The link to your picture is included with the tweet that goes out to all your followers. The subject of your email is the caption under your picture.

TIP when using TwitPic.com

Your username is the same as your Twitter ID. For example, mine is: http://twitpic.com/photos/CoachDeb

My followers get to comment on any picture I've uploaded. When they comment, it sends a message back to me instantly. They don't even have to include the usual @CoachDeb in the comment box to send it directly to me because any comment left on any of my TwitPics automatically gets sent to me, and will be seen both in my replies tab and in the comments section of the picture itself.

Timesaving hint for people who haven't used TwitPic.com yet:

Don't bother trying to "sign up" to TwitPic. There is NO "signup" tab anywhere on the site. If you're using Twitter already, you're already signed up for TwitPic.com! You just have to log in.

Simply log in using the same username and password that you used for Twitter, and you're in!

Twitter Tip:

If you're ever stuck, just ask the Twitterverse. If you don't have a big following yet, ask someone with a big following to ask their tribe the question with which you need help. They will instantly reply. It's better than Google! Especially since everybody likes to help and you give them the opportunity to contribute to your life. And that makes everybody feel good. Doesn't it?

Chapter 15

Positioning & Branding Yourself on Twitter

A pivotal day on Twitter for me personally was the time I was watching the stream in *Twhirl *(* Twitter app that remains as a column on your desktop while you work on other projects)* when a tweet caught my attention.

Since Twhirl highlights the tweets that have your username in them, I was alerted to someone talking about me.

My inquiring mind wanted to know. What question was he responding to?

His tweet started as a reply to @DaveTaylor who asked the question, "Who is really good at getting their brand out there on Twitter?"

To which this gentleman responded,

"@DaveTaylor From what I've seen @CoachDeb is really good on Twitter & is well known, respected & liked but I don't know what she's pitching."

I had mixed feelings about this reply, because on one hand, he doesn't know what I "sell" which "can't be good for business" right?

But on the OTHER hand, I'm "top of mind" and I was the first tweeter mentioned in this poll sent out by Dave Taylor who's followed by 1,933 people and counting and is well known in the community as an influencer in social media.

Positioning is all about the battle for your mind. And in an over-communicated marketplace, if you're thought of first in the mind of a potential customer, you'll get more business than you can handle.

The marketing classic book *Positioning* by Al Ries and Jack Trout discusses the power of being positioned first in the minds of your customers.

"History shows that the first brand into the brain, on the average, gets twice the long-term market share of the No. 2 brand and twice again as much as the No. 3 brand. And the relationships are not easily changed."

Here's how I look at positioning my brand on Twitter. Be forewarned, it may shock you.

The first time someone tweets me may or may not be when they find out about my optimized blogging software or consulting services. That's okay. I don't expect that to be the case.

In fact, if you want to know my secret in how I approach my online presence on Twitter and other social networks, when it comes to positioning my brand, keep reading. It's all about transparency these days right? No more secrets?

First of all, I don't view anyone as a "prospect" on Twitter. I see them first as a potential friend who may have similar interests, values, and work ethic. Perhaps they'll be a like-minded professional with whom I'll enjoy hanging out with at a conference. Perhaps the person is someone I can learn from. Or the person is an influencer who could connect me with thousands of other influencers whom I could serve.

I never really know on the first tweet. That's why I'm as involved as I am, in order to get a full picture of who's who and what's what before "rushing into a pitch."

The more you connect with the people who are following you and enter into conversations with them, the more you'll be able to connect with them and position your brand as an authentic individual who isn't just looking to be a rock star to be worshiped and followed.

I'm sharing insider secrets from within my tribe who share with me via DM how they unfollow the gurus who only want to hear the sound of their own tweet.

There are too many tweeters on twitter who follow you just so you'll follow them back, then they UNfollow you so it looks like more people follow them. (Not cool.)

The problem with this approach is that to your potential client, it looks like you really don't "listen" to anyone and would rather "do the talking." This is extremely unattractive for the female buyer who is there to develop relationships and do business with people she likes.

Again, this is not just one woman's opinion. It's based on the hundreds of women who've participated in focus groups, in addition to the dozens of DM's I get on a regular basis telling me how they feel.

If you haven't already read "Marketing to Women" by Martha Barletta, I suggest you add that to your Amazon list before you finish this chapter. It's a must read for anyone involved with social media or marketing in this century. (Think this means you?)

It's the interactions and conversations you have with people that will attract a much larger following where you'll build your own tribe, as opposed to those on Twitter who don't interact with their followers.

Don't take my word for it. Do the math. Robert Scoble @Scobleizer attracted 30,000 followers because he is social and interacts on Twitter. He also generates conversation. And when he tweets, people listen and interact back to him.

Warren @WarrenWhitlock attracted over 3,000 followers within three months because he engaged with people. He followed people back, watched the conversation and provided valuable resources which caused other people to retweet him and therefore attract additional followers.

The bottom line is, if you want to be listened to, then do a little listening and interacting.

People will see you having conversations with others. If they like what you have to say and are intrigued with the questions and comments you contribute, they will connect with you and form lasting bonds that won't easily be broken.

Remember, people do business with people, not brands or companies. However, the more they respect you and the brand you stand for, the better positioned you'll be in their mind when they're ready to do business with you.

Twitter cuts through all of the phony attempts of companies making business sterile and makes business personal and fun again!

There is no line any more between your professional persona and your personal brand.

The more authentic you are, even if it means disagreeing with some to attract others, the more you'll be respected.

People need to think about new media marketing, often called "social media," very differently than what they were taught in business school. There is no line between business and personal anymore. That's the approach large companies take to protect anything from leaking to shareholders.

Blogging, YouTube videos, Ustream channels, and Twitter each allow people to share who they really are with their viewers.

Ask yourself:

"Who am I really? What message do I want to get across?"

Another difference when positioning yourself on Twitter is that there is no longer any privacy. Privacy is another dead concept when it comes to new media marketing. It's all about transparency and authenticity.

There's such a blurred line now between your business and personal life. It gets back to that model that business is *always* personal. The more you make it so, the more you'll connect with people who need, want, and desire your services.

Chapter 16

Marketing Yourself on Twitter & Connecting with Influencers

All this is great and interesting, but do people actually make money on Twitter?

How are businesses converting their tweets into dollars?

Prepare for a little shock and awe. Because making money on Twitter is different than typical network marketing and opposite of anything you've ever learned about internet marketing.

But if you engage properly in this new trend, you'll attract, connect, and convert people easier and better than you've ever done before Twitter was born.

Rather than follow the rules of traditional in-person networking tactics that don't work, I do the exact opposite.

Old fashioned marketing taught you to walk up to someone new at a networking event, shake their hand, look squarely into the person's eyes and, share your 60-minute elevator speech (or USP—unique selling proposition) in order to make connections.

Whereas on Twitter, the way people find out about what I do is follow the trail. Essentially they "discover" what I do, after they learn who "I am."

Exact Steps of How I "Market" on Twitter

Here's the trail of how a tweet turns into cold hard cash:

Let's take @ MarieLCoccia as an example.

I tweet a new media marketing tip.

Marie likes it.

Marie follows me.

She observes the chats I have about everything from politics to business, and all the messy stuff in between.

She participates in the conversation. I reply back.

She then starts tracking the conversations I have with other clients, fans, and followers who rave about the blogging system our company created, by following my username in the Twummize.com stream.

She's impressed.

She checks it out.

(Note: Some tweeters ask outright what it is that I do. While others simply click on my profile, see the link to my blog, and check out what I do subtly.)

One day, Marie clicks on my blog. She now gets to know me as a recognized expert and authority in new media marketing and tribal marketing through our blog TribalSeduction.com.

Then she notices a subtle little ad for my 1st book on new media marketing *Secrets of Online Persuasion*. She orders it through Amazon.

In the meantime, I give her a compelling reason to subscribe to my blog, and stay in touch.

While leaving a comment on our blog one sunny afternoon, she notices the subtle, little ad on the side of our blog about the blogging software that works FOR you.

Marie is now intrigued.

She clicks on the link.

She watches our video from the comfort of her own home or office. She hears us explain how this new media marketing hub site will automate much of her social marketing efforts.

Marie likes what she sees, because it's relevant to her needs.

Keep in mind, throughout this entire process, it's all "passive" marketing. She's never picked up the phone to have a chat with me, or asked me what my "USP" is. Rather she gets to screen me in decide if it's something she needs, wants or desires.

There is zero pressure in this style of "Discovery Marketing". Whether she ever becomes a client or not is irrelevant to me, because she's a great person to talk with during my work breaks.

But she likes what she sees, and she clicks to order the software.

A sale is made without me ever having to pick up the phone and make a cold call, warm call or sales call. Sure we've chatted, but it's never been about "what I can do for her business." It's always personal (or politics.)

Marie sends me an @CoachDeb message and tells me she just became a member.

I send her an @ reply back and celebrate her decision.

For anyone who thinks Twitter is a waste of time, and not where business is done, is simply not doing it right! I'll do this every day and twice on Sunday if it means all I need to do is be myself, and socialize on the net, and allow people to decide whether I've got what they need, instead of me having to chase anyone down.

No thank you. I'll take Twitter instead, please.

In an age of permission marketing, as Seth Godin predicted back in the 90's with his book *Permission Marketing*, it's all about keeping your brand in front of your clients so you're top of mind, and they ask YOU what you do rather than you making a cold-call to try to hock what you've got.

I haven't made one sales call ever since I've been on Twitter. Not a single one. People pursue me as a result of being positioned in their mind as an expert and an authority in new media marketing.

How can you beat that?!

Social Media Marketing TIP for your Profile page:

Do not put a sales page up as your link from your profile. Use a blog hub site instead.

You get a limited amount of space for your profile on Twitter. Don't use a sales page or landing page where people have to "opt in" in order to get to know you. That is so Web 1.0. It is NOT new media marketing and it's certainly not "social marketing" by a long stretch!

You'll get far better results by linking to your blog where they can get to know you better.

Think about the word "congruency" and write it down in the margins of this book.

Your goal is to be congruent with your tweeting and with your new media marketing strategy.

If you're having a conversation over on Twitter, it's a social media venue. People are getting to know you *personally*. If you automatically send them to a sales letter, it's incongruent. It stops the conversation dead in its tracks.

I guarantee there will still be internet marketers who will tell you, "Landing pages work! Look at my numbers!"

But what the guru doesn't tell you is that the numbers of sign ups they get are there because of their reputation as gurus, not because of the method they used for collecting names for their list.

It works for "the big names" in spite of the method. But for the person who is just getting started out on Twitter and social media marketing and doesn't have a big name yet, landing pages are a turnoff to those participating on Twitter just like you. (Not to mention that landing pages are not Google-friendly.)

Google Insider, Simon Leung, co-founder of the Google AdWords Optimization Team and former Sr. AdWords Optimization Specialist who developed the strategies and trainings for Google employees still taught today, revealed to us:

"Google views social media sites as high authority sites, and therefore ranks them higher than static Web sites and sales pages, because it's where people are actively participating and interacting."

You can follow him @SimonLeung and subscribe to his popular blog at http://SimonLeung.com

That's why when you do a search on our names "Coach Deb" or "Warren Whitlock" you'll see our tweets show up, because Google sees Twitter as highly relevant to the conversations happening right now.

When you link to a blog from your Twitter profile, you're using a congruent channel. You start a conversation on Twitter, then your visitor goes over to your blog and thinks, "Good! I can continue the conversation here."

Social Media Marketing TIP for your Tweets:

Please don't publish a new blog post, and tweet, a boring tweet like: "Here's the link." Give your followers a compelling reason to click on your link and check out your blog.

Remember, people are busy. But they won't be able to resist checking out a link if you tell them how the information impacts them in their business or life.

Unless you've already got your clients following you who expect and want to know the instant you've published a new blog post, the average tweeter coming across that tweet will simply ignore that tweet.

Whereas, when you tweet something intriguing, captivating, provocative, or seductive, people will not be able to resist clicking on your link!

Tell your reader WHY they should click on your link. Don't just tell them you put a new blog post up. Who cares? I certainly don't care, and the Twitterverse doesn't care. We don't have the time to click on every little link someone shares.

However, if you tweet an intriguing question along with the direct link to your post, something like, "Who do you think is better at social marketing: men or women? Be the first to comment." You'll have dozens of followers clicking over to your post immediately so they can comment on your blog (depending on the time of day you tweet).

Oh yeah, that's another great side benefit of Twitter—getting more traffic to your blog!

REMEMBER: You will get much higher click-throughs if you captivate your reader and use influential language.

This is a 180-degree turn from what a lot of people teach in the internet marketing world. I understand that it may be a little bit controversial and may create some great debate in Twitter or on the online Twitter Handbook http://TwitterHandbook.com but that's what Twitter is all about. The conversation.

Do not be afraid of the debate and controversy on Twitter. It's a great attraction and influence tool. But that's for the next chapter.

Chapter 17

When & How to "Talk Business" on Twitter

The Companies Doing it Right

The more popular Twitter becomes, the more corporations are going to realize they need to have a presence in social media and will need to track their brand.

There are several early-adopter large corporations who are doing a great job on Twitter marketing their company, products, or services without being perceived as "spammy" or ad-driven.

A few examples of some large companies to check out on Twitter that are doing it right are @Zappos, @ComcastCares and @JetBlue.

Zappos is a shoe company. If you've been reading this book as a retail store owner and been thinking, "How can I sell my products on Twitter?" You're reading the right chapter! Zappos has figured out a way to sell more that's as entertaining and engaging as the people managing their Twitter account.

One of the best marketing strategies Zappos uses on Twitter is holding contests.

**Write this down:
Contests are the new advertising.**

Hold contests. It's a brilliant way to get people involved and get them to spread the word about your company. People love getting stuff for free, especially if it's something they want.

And what woman doesn't like shoes?

Zappos.com has been phenomenal at getting their tribe drooling and waiting for the moment they're going to tweet.

The other night I even participated when I was online and saw his tweet come in saying, "Okay, contest is ON! The first person who tweets @Zappos with their favorite brand of shoe sold on Zappos.com gets a pair FREE!"

Voila! Instantly, they got dozens of @ replies because people were waiting for that moment, having seen an earlier tweet telling them that within the next 3 hours they would be giving away a free pair of shoes to the first person who answers their tweet.

Now THAT's an effective way of "creating the drool" for your product or service. Not to mention to remain "top of mind" in the minds of your customers for the evening!

Dave Lakhani, who did the foreword for our book *Secrets of Online Persuasion,* is a guru in influence and persuasion. He's been in a cult, and has a very interesting background that not many business owners have. He also has police and military training.

Coach Deb spoke at his event, Renegades of Persuasion, talking about Twitter and new media marketing. Dave is brilliant at getting his tribe waiting and drooling on Twitter when he has events.

His followers wait for him to tweet, standing by for hours just to get his new book, "Subliminal Persuasion" when he tweets live on stage when traveling around the world speaking. Check out

@DaveLakhani's Twitter profile to see how he uses subliminal persuasion in the way he Tweets as a great example to model.

If you've got something your clients want, they'll work a little for a contest. And in the meantime, your costs are minimal to manage a contest.

Whether it's a pair of shoes or a book, you'll have dozens if not hundreds of tweeters on the edge of their seats hoping that this time, they'll win your contest—all the while, thinking about you and your products.

Tip to Use Twitter Influentially:
If you don't know much about influence and persuasion, you need to improve that skill. It's THE most important skill set to have on Twitter or any other social media site.

That's what it's all about on twitter. It's not about marketing. It's about being persuasive and seductive and being an influencer.

Chapter 18

Twetiquette & Reputation Management

Think before you tweet. After all, you never know what kind of an influencer is behind the curtain of a username.

You can do a lot of damage to your reputation if you don't realize the power of language.

Just because you may be sitting behind the barrier of a computer instead of being face to face with someone, be careful of what you tweet—especially if it's negative about anyone.

I'm always in shock when I see Twossip (Gossip on Twitter). I think, "Don't they realize others can read what they tweet?" You're not just telling your followers, you're telling the entire world, because your tweets turn into separate Web pages— available to the general public doing a search on your name or the keywords you're using.

So be careful what you tweet.

We've already talked about reputation management as it has to do with the Twitter Trolls in an earlier chapter.

Be sure to be using Google Alerts to track your name, your company's name, and any products or services you promote in order to see if anyone is using your brand improperly.

One thing we haven't addressed yet that is important is someone trying to use your name that isn't you. This goes against Twitter's TOS (Terms of Service.) Not to mention it is illegal for your trademarked products or services.

However it's up to you to do something about it. This is one of the biggest reasons why reputation management positions are becoming one of the fastest new positions being created and filled by corporations today. As companies are learning about the power of new media and social networks like Twitter, Facebook, MySpace, etc. they're realizing they need to have someone manage this activity for them.

The Twitter squatter is someone who grabs your name because they know your name or company has a draw in and of itself. They may or may not be tweeting from your name, but you have the right to your name and the right to take it over. You just need to take action in order to protect your reputation from people tweeting things in your name that you don't stand behind.

I've seen people do this for the internet marketing gurus. They'll grab the guru's name, sit on it, and not do anything with it.

Those who try to tweet using the guru's name are beyond Twitter squatters and are Twitter Trolls and brand-jackers. Read about them in section one of this book. It's a more involved process in reputation management.

If anyone has grabbed your name and isn't using it or they're trying to use it and they're not you, you can contact Twitter. You can send a message to @Twitter, and submit a ticket at http://help.twitter.com

Let Twitter know somebody is squatting on your name and they will give it to you. It may take a few days, but persist on getting this taken care of.

This worked very easily for my friend, @Shane whose twitter squatter hadn't tweeted from the name in over a year.

So when I noticed someone was sitting on my friend John Reese's name, I passed on the tip.

When John Reese first joined Twitter, he was forced to use the underscore in between his name because someone already grabbed his name, knowing he's a popular internet marketer whose name alone would draw followers searching for him on Twitter.

John Reese is one of the internet marketing gurus who uses Twitter right. Despite getting a lot of heat from the popular @mashable blog for bringing thousands of people onto twitter who were taught his traffic secrets, ever since John's first tweet he's been doing it right.

He interacts with his followers, follows people back, shares funny moments from his summer vacation in Greece that are highly entertaining and engaging, and participates in the conversation when he's not riding on his moped getting himself in trouble with the local police.

It took a few weeks for John Reese to get his name from the Twitter squatter after reporting it. But all of a sudden, it just appeared as his username. He got his name sans underscore. Horrray!

USERNAME TIP: When this happens, be sure to go in and quickly grab your name WITH the underscore back under a different email account, so that all the links you've already created from your tweets WITH the underscore won't be broken, and you won't have another twitter squatter grabbing THAT name.

ANONYMITY on the net

It's interesting how "anonymity" emboldens people to say things they'd never say to your face if they were talking to you in-person.

Try not to take things personally. And if someone disrespects you or treats you badly, do what I do—tweet about it!

You'll not only feel better through the cathartic process of sharing your frustration, hurt, or disappointment. You'll also be uplifted by the overwhelming support from your true loyal followers.

Let them lift you up when you're feeling down. You'll build a true bond with tweeples when you allow this to happen naturally.

Here's a tweet from one of my followers when I shared something someone said that bothered me.

@CoachDeb some dudes find it easy to be bold behind a keyboard. Face to face, they're not so tuff

2 minutes ago from twhirl in reply to CoachDeb

Jim Turner

Jim really encouraged me when he shared this on Twitter.

And remember before you blast someone on Twitter, keep in mind that there's a real person behind the computer screen that you may be hurting. Someone's mom, sister, brother, dad, or child.

So think before you tweet. After all, you never know what kind of an influencer is behind the curtain of a username.

Using Twitter for Chat

Just so you know, it's perfectly okay to use Twitter for chat. I've heard people say, "Why do people use Twitter for chat? Twitter is not for chat." I know I've given you some "don't" tips here, but here's another "don't" that might boggle your mind. Don't listen to the people who are telling you not to use Twitter for X, Y, and Z. Use it how you want.

Just remember where the advice is coming from and how they're able to build a tribe. You do want to be influencing and persuading. If you keep that in mind, the tip is either good or bad based on, "Will this tip help me make connections? Will it help me attract and connect with people?" That's the winning formula to abide by.

If you tend to tweet a lot, have two separate accounts so one can be the one where they have mobile notifications on. That's why @CoachDeb uses @DeborahMicek as her quiet profile that follows only the people she actively does business with. That's where her clients know she barely tweets once a week—IF that! It might be once a day, but it's not going to be the 10 or 20 times a day that @CoachDeb can easily tweet.

Be "mobile phone follow-worthy". Be a tweeter who's worthy of not only being followed, but being turned on.

Chapter 19

Attract, Connect, & Convert Raving Fans

Whether you're heavily involved in politics in Washington DC, or running a family-owned shrimp shack on the north shore of Hawaii in the middle of the Pacific, Twitter is your new tool in attracting new fans who follow you. Even if you're not a Hollywood celebrity!

There are many ways to do attract and connect with your followers, but for a moment, I'd like to cover a controversial approach to attracting raving fans who'll follow you to the end of the earth.

Turn someone off.

You read me right. Turn a few tweeters off to you and your tweets by being authentic and radically transparent.

Now we've already discussed twetiquette. So you know how to treat people well through your tweets. Assuming you know how to disagree and still be diplomatic about it, go ahead and turn some people off by expressing your true opinions on things.

Erin Kotecki Vest (@QueenofSpain) does this all the time on Twitter. Producer for BlogHer.com as well as contributing regularly to the Huffington Post, MOMocrats.com, Erin has made her opinions known about her choice in presidential candidates from day one. Regardless of how many tweeters don't agree with her endorsement of Obama, it hasn't stopped her from attracting 3,745 followers at the time of this writing. She's active, she expresses her political beliefs, and she makes no bones about doing so. The Momocrats who follow her love her because of this. That's her tribe, and she's sticking to it.

Then you have the direct "opposite" of Erin on Twitter with Lauren Goddard, (@LGoddard), who is so bold about sharing her political beliefs that she includes this in her profile box: "I'm a Republican and proud of it." She doesn't mind if people who are die-hard Democrats don't like her because she's a Republican. She's not changing her beliefs, so it's better they find out right from the get-go. But by boldly stating her beliefs, Lauren has attracted strong Republicans and even some closet Republicans who were afraid of talking politics on Twitter which began in the tech-community, which tends to be full of Democrats.

Influence Tip:

Write this down in your own handwriting in the margins of this page:

Polarized tweeters are buyers.

You don't necessarily have to get involved in world politics to be controversial either.

It could be the battle of the sexes, religion, or who you're going to vote for on American Idol.

The bottom line is that when you are authentic and radically transparent in your beliefs, you'll gain the respect of others who appreciate the fact that they know where you stand.

They may not agree with you, but they'll enjoy following you because they love getting involved with healthy debate.

Don't be afraid of debate. Just be diplomatic about it.

And don't worry when some intolerant people unfollow you because they don't share your opinion or beliefs. Just like in life, some people only want to surround themselves with people who think just like them.

That's okay. Clients will find out about your value system sooner or later so it might as well be sooner so you know you're attracting a potential raving fan in all areas of your life.

This may or may not be a strategy you're comfortable with. That's okay too. There are plenty of other gentler approaches to attracting and connecting with your followers.

But for those who are bold enough to go where no tweeter has gone before...okay well, that's not true. In fact, we've seen more evidence to the intense activity that debate creates, bringing the topic of discussion to #1 on trending topics on Search.Twitter.com

So, only one question remains—can you handle the truth?

CONTROVERSY:
to be or not to be controversial or political in your tweets

Controversy sells.

Controversy repels.

Controversy attracts.

People are much more likely to get involved in a discussion that actually means something, especially if they're passionate about it.

The #DontGo movement http://DontGoMovement.com is a perfect example of this fact.

It began one hot summer day on The Hill (Capitol Hill in America) when one lonely tweeter in Washington got a flood of followers in one day after mainstream media cut off their television syndication feed to the American people watching from their TV's at home.

The debate started over whether Congress should take a 5 week summer vacation or stay and work on The American Energy Act to address the high price of gas affecting all American families.

It was one of the first times we were not only seeing politicians use Twitter personally while they were working, but seeing a firestorm of controversy and support all at the same time after mainstream media could no longer broadcast from The Hill.

Speaker of the House, Nancy Pelosi turned off the lights hoping congress men and women would just go home and enjoy a 5-week vacation.

But when Republicans kept their conversation going in the dark, she turned off their microphones in an attempt to silence the people.

CSPAN (traditional media) could no longer broadcast when the lights and mics went out in Washington. But that didn't stop @JohnCulberson from tweeting from his mobile phone (new media). The only voice that was able to communicate to the people what was going on was one tweeter texting from his mobile phone.

Once word got out, the American people spread the word like wild fire via Twitter. A basic Web site was created where the American people could express their opinion by adding their names to Call Congress Back http://CallCongressBack.com which got thousands of votes within 24 hours of the first tweet from inside the Capitol building from Congressman @JohnCulberson.

Trending topics:
- #dontgo
- Paris Hilton
- iPhone
- McCain
- Apple
- The Dark Knight
- Obama
- AT&T
- National Night Out
- Beijing

#DontGo remained the #1 trending topic on Twitter for an entire week while Congress was "unofficially" in session, with politicians tweeting and the American people tweeting back, getting engaged in the debate and following the Don't Go Movement from their cell phones and internet using Twemes to track the conversation: http://twemes.com/dontgo

All this resulted in over 34,369 votes to date at the time of this writing, just weeks after the @DontGo Movement began. DontGoMovement.com

While you may risk losing a few intolerant followers who won't listen to alternative points of views, you'll attract a flood of tweeters who think just like you. This is where true attraction and ultimate connection occurs.

Whether you're tweeting about Barack Hussein Obama, currently running for US Presidency or his Republican opponent, John Sidney McCain III, you'll attract some while polarizing others. Test this and see. The mere mention of their names will attract a flood of @ replies especially if you take a stand one way or the other.

It's perfectly acceptable to debate on Twitter, just as long as you're not name-calling or acting like a child. That's what will not only lose you followers, but it'll lose you respect and damage your reputation as well.

PROVIDE VALUE

When you provide value in your tweets, you'll force your followers to pay attention to you when you tweet.

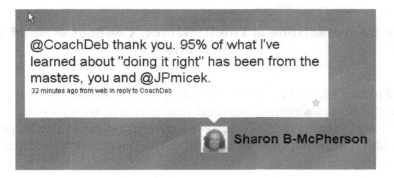

@CoachDeb thank you. 95% of what I've learned about "doing it right" has been from the masters, you and @JPmicek.

32 minutes ago from web in reply to CoachDeb

Sharon B-McPherson

I don't just willy-nilly tweet, even though people see me tweeting fast and furious. I'm always very cognizant of "Is this tweet-worthy?" Sometimes I have to resist sending an @ reply. I really want to, but I don't want to tweet all that much and have people then un-follow me. I'll often send the person a DM (direct message) in order to let them know I hear them, and reply to their tweet.

I had a few guys in the beginning who tweeted at me, "That's too much," and I thought to myself, "Okeedookee then. Unfollow me. My tribe likes my tips, quips, and humor. If you don't like it, you shouldn't be following me."

Then I'd look at Robert Scoble, and how he puts up with people picking on him for being "noisy" on Twitter and realize, it doesn't bother him; and he's successfully attracted over 30,000 followers by *being* noisy, so it shouldn't bother me, and it certainly shouldn't stop me. Or you!

It's interesting. There will be people who don't understand the power of chatting on Twitter and connecting with people. But that's what it's all about. **It's about the conversation.**

Ignore the critics. Do what you know is right for your tribe. Provide value and benefit to the tribe. Do that and you will attract and connect with a flood of followers.

Have Conversations & You'll Attract, Connect & Bond with Your Tribe

Jeff Turner (@ResPres) the President and Founder of RealEstateShows.com described this concept well in the ActiveRain forum, (http://activerain.com/respres) the largest real estate network online, and with his permission, I share his post with you here:

It's not about what you're doing.
It's not about what I'm doing.
It's about what you and I are doing *right now.*

Like you, I didn't get twitter either. I was trying to make it something it wasn't and it's just not that complicated.

It's about the conversation.

It doesn't matter whether it's here on ActiveRain or on Twitter. You, of all people, should know that.

Is there a lot of silly conversation on Twitter? Sure. There's a lot of silly conversation here too. That happens on social networks. It's how people get to know each other.

If it weren't for the silly conversations, the completely "meaningless" banter, you and I would not be as close as we are. If it weren't for the silly conversations, the off-topic hijacks, you and I would not be as close as we are. It's SOCIAL media. It's about being social. It's not about Google juice or SEO. It's not meant to be purely about business. It's social.

Twitter is about the conversation. Period.

Chapter 20

The Seduction of Twitter

Follow Me.

Do you ever feel like people are following you?

Well if you're on Twitter your paranoia would be justified.

There is a voyeur in each of us on Twitter. We don't always engage in the conversation.

Sometimes, we just watch.

We see who's talking to who. Who's talking @ who, and through all of these observations, you can easily detect who is an influencer on Twitter, who is a wanna-be, and who is someone you should steer clear of!

It's all about The Tribal Factor with Twitter.

New lingo, followers, apps, words no one else knows outside the tribe, customs and jokes only tweeters can understand—all these things work to create a powerful tribal factor that is Twitter.

Mobile Marketing Joke: Mr Online and Mr Offline are
sitting in a bar...

MOBILE MARKETING

Mr Online and Mr Offline are sitting in a bar discussing
their various marketing tactics when in walks the
young, voluptuous Miss Mobile; after a few drinks they
strike up a conversation.

*"Hey, why not come over to Myspace and we can
Google together"* says Mr. Online. Immediately Mr.
Offline pipes in, *"Hey, forget that, I can get you on
billboards or perhaps a magazine spread."*

Totally unimpressed, Miss Mobile strolls to the door,
turning to say, *"Sorry guys, it sounds like neither of
you are in to TEXT."*

*Follow Dan Hollings
twitter.com/dhollings*

(Contributed by Dan Hollings @Dhollings with permission)

Bios and How We Speak has Drastically Changed

Remember how bios used to be written in third person?
"Warren is _____. He has _____." Now, that's old-school.

On Twitter, you write your bio in first person. On your About Us
page of your blog, share your story.

Don't use the traditional third-person bio. Save that for
Corporate America, Fortune 500 companies, the government, or
politicians who are asking for your consulting services. Save
that third-person bio for when they need to introduce you when
presenting from the stage or at a company meeting.

When people are connecting with you on your blog or Web site,
have an About Me page in a story-like fashion to influence
people and persuade them to follow you, not just to be
impressed by you.

Tribal Seduction Tip:

Think of both Twitter (your micro-blog) and your blog hub site as having a one-to-one conversation. I don't care that 200 people are reading your blog post or tweet at this very moment. When you write or tweet, talk to one person.

Let's look at a tweet for comparison purposes so you can see the difference.

When you ask a question in a tweet, instead of writing, "What does *everyone* think about Obama?" tweet as though you're asking only one person, "What do you think about Obama?"

Do you see the difference?

Tribal Social Networks Have Emerged

Sites like **Flikr** are a perfect example of the tribal nature of online social networks to bring like-minded individuals together around similar interests.

Fellow tweeter Joe Philipson, @Jphilipson, is a photographer here in Hawaii who immediately started doing more business with the people he met and connected with on Twitter.

He's also an active user of http://Flickr.com which I'll let him describe to you so you can get a feel for how this trend of social media and tribal marketing will be the norm in the 21st Century:

"Flickr is an example of what I call a 'specified social network.' A specified social network is a network that is built around a sub-culture of people rather than a larger community of people such as MySpace or Facebook. This type of network can be built around specific interests or hobbies. Flickr started as a site to upload and share photos with friends and families but has turned into a social network for aspiring amateur photographers and professional photographers alike."

Twitter appeals to all personality types but some more than others for different reasons.

Social Media is the most ironic term that's ever hit the new media landscape.

It makes sense that introverts would love tools like Twitter because it allows them to reveal their true self, but only AFTER a little thoughtful consideration. That's hard to do face-to-face without the long, dramatic pause, making the whole situation a very awkward conversation to say the least.

You can easily observe and classify who is an introvert or extrovert by their tweets.

For example:

Extroverts will tend to have fast tweets coming rapid fire, with mis-spellings up the wazoo, and not give a hoot about "the details."

Introverts on the other hand will delay their tweet, re-read their tweet, correct their tweet, and often revise their tweet until it's "just right."

The best thing about online networking is that behavior through communication is easily observable, and therefore, classifiable. This gives you the insider knowledge on how to communicate with someone who is interested in your products or services— all based on the clues they've given you in their Twitter stream.

Go check it out. I promise, you'll never look at a tweet the same again without seeing a clue here or there based on this information. Every tweet reveals what type of person is "behind the mask" at their desk (or in front of their phone, as the case might be.)

The more knowledgeable you are in the areas of persuasion and influence the more you'll know exactly what a tweeter's hot buttons are.

Develop Thick Skin as you attract your tribe

When I was first getting involved with Twitter, learning the ropes, seeing how people were using the @ symbol to have conversations with one another, someone publicly tweeted @ me announcing they were unfollowing me because I was using Twitter to have conversations.

As a Jersey-girl, I'm not supposed to admit that stung just a bit. (So I won't.)

It was the first negative tweet I had seen and I thought, "Is this too much?"

It's natural to doubt yourself when you're first starting out. It's all new so you think, "Am I doing it wrong?"

In an effort to understand what Twitterverse protocol was, and see what my own tribe of followers wanted, I tweeted what this guy had rudely said to me.

About 35 people instantly replied, telling me why they loved following me and what they liked about my tweets. Some people gave me specific things they liked about my tweets. I thought, "Wow, there's a formula in there of what they're sharing. That is actually what I'm doing—without even realizing it!"

Someone tweeted @ me giving me feedback that I provide valuable resources and am funny. Funny is a fundamental of my personality, so their tweet put a smile on my face. Some tweets of mine are simply me just being me, either being entertaining or making someone laugh or feel good. It's what I enjoy doing "in the real world" so it's only natural that I do the same on Twitter.

Someone sent me a screen shot to prove it wasn't just their opinion but that I had attained #3 in the top ten list for "funny tweeters in the past 14 days."

Funny people, past 14 days	
58	erwblo
56	marketingfacts
50	coachdeb
45	rotjong
40	isheila
40	puur
39	jojanneke
39	markies
37	msh2006
36	frankmeeuwsen

I've gotta say, that chart made my day! And I promptly grabbed a screen shot of the list and planted it on my partner's desk. (AKA: @JPMicek)

"People think I'm funny!" I told my partner in crime. Then I pointed to my name saying, "Seeeeee? Now you've gotta laugh at my silly jokes!"

Oh he laughed at that alright! But I have a sneaking suspicion that he was lauging @ me, not with me. Hmmm... I just wish he appreciated my humor as much as my tweeples do!

My followers mentioned a few other things I did in regards to keeping them informed of what's happening both in current events in the world as well as trends in social media.

It was great feedback for me to find out why people were following me, and what they expected from me. It's a great thing for you to do too—get feedback from your followers. Go ahead and do that from time to time. Use Twitter as your focus group to get feedback on anything.

All of my tweets fall into five categories. I recommend that each of you have five specific things that you tweet about. For me, I try to be funny in some of my tweets. But if you're not funny, don't try to be something you're not. (Btw: Please don't @ me to tell me I'm not funny. Someone said on Twitter that I'm funny, so that's it. That's my story and I'm sticking to it.)

Be whatever your personality is. Then think about a tip you're going to provide in your industry. Think of three other ways you can tweet. Every five tweets, you can rotate this formula. No need to be strict about it, just think about this as your guide. There might be 10 tweets that are interactive and chat-worthy. Get that ratio of a 1-to-10 or 1-to-8 of interjecting a resource in the midst of your conversations with other tweeters.

When I have chats back and forth I'll make sure I throw out a tip for anyone who gets tired of my "noise." (Note: A lot of tweets back and forth are what they call "noise" on twitter.) If it ever gets to be a one-on-one chat, I'll take it to DM, and then IM with that person.

Be sure you tweet something of value in the midst of any conversation you may be having with your active followers.

Share a tip a day in your niche.

I was talking to Sherman Hu the other day (@ShermanHu). He asked me in a DM, "What do you think about my Twitter stream? Why do you follow me?"

I tweeted back, "What I love most about following you is the techy tips you share. I'm not that geeky. I need those techy tips to expand my knowledge."

My favorite tweet of Hu's thus far is when he shared this really cool article about a hologram presenter and the wave of the future for bringing the classroom to your computer.

If you can be the first to let people know about cool technology, you will be a valuable resource, and remembered. Think about that when you're tweeting and strive to be RE-tweet-worthy.

That's when someone retweets something you just tweeted because it was oh-so-good!

Remember to give credit where credit is due.

Tweets serve as timelines and permanent records. Don't just copy what someone shared without mentioning where you picked it up and who shared the resource first with you.

And if someone is ganging up on you, let your Twitter followers know. They will rise up in your defense, and become a stronger tribe as a result. It felt so good when I connected with my tweeple when someone was picking on me.

Now I can do the same for my friends when they reach the pinnacle of success to be worthy of attracting annoying people.

Now when jealous attackers or so-called-competitors come up on my Twitter stream, I simply let my friends come to my defense. And when they do, my bond with my followers grows deeper.

I find I pay attention to their tweets more, because they were there for me in my time of need.

Be follow-worthy with every tweet, and you'll easily succeed on Twitter.

CHAPTER 21

Influencing the Influencers & Attracting your Choice Client

Contributed by @JPmicek with permission from his popular blog: TribalSeduction.com

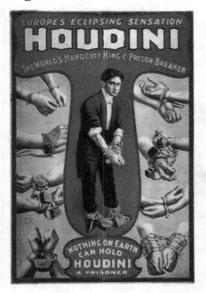

What's the secret to attracting attention and winning over people's hearts, minds and pocketbooks? It's the ability to influence and persuade. It's what all business owners, sales pros and politicians want -- but most start from the wrong place

Persuasion start with Self-Influence™

Mention persuasion to the average person and ask them where persuasion is focused -- outward (on other people) or inward.

99 out of 100 will say "on other people." After all, isn't the idea

to win friends and influence people? Isn't that what we should be focused on?

Yeah, sure - that's the ultimate goal. But unless you master Self-Influence™ your persuasion skills will always come across as mechanical, un-natural.

Think about it. If you can't influence and motivate yourself to take action -- how can you ever effectively motivate anyone else?

The fact is you won't. People's perception will immediately be one of suspicion. Not a good place to start a relationship, I'm sure you agree.

Have you ever heard of Harry Houdini?

Well he wasn't like today's magicians, only interested in filling a theatre in Vegas. He was an artist. He could make an elephant disappear in the middle of a theatre filled with people, and do you know how he did that?

By controlling people's perceptions.

...What the eyes see and the ears hear, the mind believes. Perception is reality.

Until you control people's perception of you, your brand, your persona, and who you really are at your core – you will never attain the levels of influence and persuasion that you want. And yes, that applies online too because there is NO hiding behind your screen. Not anymore!

Photo by White Studio.

Online persuasion

It's easy to see influence and persuasion at work in the off-line world. You meet people and immediately begin either building or breaking rapport with your first face-to-face meeting. You've got all five senses working for you.

At first glance online persuasion of that same level may appear to be a near impossible goal. At best, most people see online persuasion as a process of mechanical manipulation; tricks and black-hat triggers used to induce people to hand over their cash.

If we were still living in the online world of Web 1.0, true online persuasion would be difficult. That was an online world where conversations were limited, and being a Marketplace Molester was the bastardized definition of begin "persuasive."

But have you noticed that going online is a different type of experience today?

With the New Media marketplace powered by people and participation, a more natural form of persuasion can be employed. Audio and video along with instant interaction and ongoing conversations simply make online persuasion another dimension of the off-line face-to-face world.

"The catch"

Online or offline -- you can't just jump in and start trying to influence others. That's like building a pyramid from the top down.

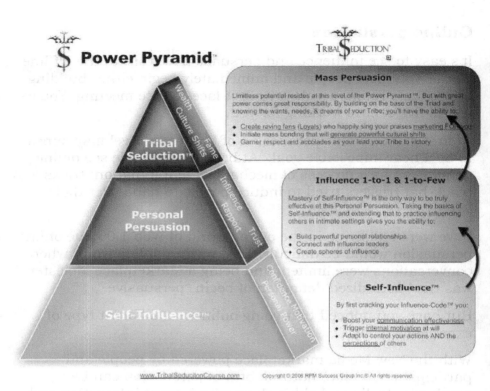

For a full-size printer-friendly PDF version of the Tribal Seduction Power Pyramid™, download it at
http://tribalseduction.com/blog/uploaded/downloads/powerpyramid.pdf

Far too many people start from the wrong place and fail to establish the foundation that will support their successfully persuading an ever growing Tribe in today's marketplace.

You need to start from the bottom up, inside out.

Here's why…

The most powerful persuasion is perceived as natural because it's seen as authentic.

If you want people to trust you and fall under your spell, it's not about "making up" a persona or image. You need to take your strengths and the magnetic aspects of your persona and make them larger than life.

To maximize your ability to persuade in marketing, sales, management, or any area of life – that means starting with understanding your natural communication style.

We each have our own unique Communication Code™. That code determines how we communicate with the outside world, how others perceive us, and how we talk to ourselves. It's an essential element in the Self-Influence™ formula. And it's the easiest place to start.

The good thing is that, when it comes to your natural communication style, you can adapt. And that ability to adapt gives you control. Control over how others perceive you, and control over how you manage and motivate yourself.

The better you understand yourself, the better you will be at getting what you want. In fact, what you don't know about yourself could keep you from getting what you want.

Today's New Media Marketplace isn't Romper Room

Focusing on Self-Influence™ first takes patience and maturity. It's not for everyone. It's a matter of doing things a little differently to make a LOT more money.

Some people are still looking for the easy way to riches. The magic bullet or secret potion. And that's ok for people who want to end up struggling and eeking out a living waiting for that pie-in-the-sky payday.

But if you're serious about achieving the wealth and lifestyle you want, sorry – <u>playtime is over</u>!

Houdini used Self-Influence™ to survive his life-threatening illusions and win over the world. Moguls like Oprah and Trump have mastered it. Branding power-houses like Gene Simmons and thought leaders Seth Godin know it, live it and profit from it.

They all know their practical strengths, Communication and Motivation Codes™. They mastered Self-Influence™ long ago and excel at persuading though perception... the reason they are where they are today.

Chapter 22

Split-Second Connections for PR

Welcome to the world's largest and longest-lasting cocktail party—all happening online and on mobile phones around the world!

In the age of speed, we've got to get connected, be connected, and stay connected; and we've got to do it fast!

Twitter has become that tool that has revolutionized the way we do business and market online in this new communication age.

Whether you're a realtor, financial advisor, politician, educator, business owner, entrepreneur, sales professional, network marketer, non-profit charity director or cruise director; Twitter is the best PR tool you can have in your pocket for instant connections.

Wendy Kurtz, PR guru residing and tweeting from Florida, shares these two tips about how "Online is Forever":

 wkurtz 1. Be conscious of fact anything you post is reflection of you/your business. One snide comment could cost you down the road. 22 minutes ago reply

wkurtz none written but could certainly do something for you...when's your deadline? I'm headed to title co. to drop off $ for new house 24 minutes ago reply

Twitter IS PR

PR = public relations. What could be a better tool than Twitter?

We interviewed PR strategist, Nancy Marmolejo from www.VivaVisibilityBlog.com who is an expert in getting free PR with numerous media outlets including SmartMoney.com, Latina magazine, Univisión TV, Redbook, and many more.

Nancy summed it up perfectly, *"If you want to get consistently called upon for expert commentary, you need to speak in catchy sound bites. What better place to practice than the quick pitch social networking worlds of Twitter and Facebook?"*

With her permission, Nancy shared these tips on Twitter PR.

Follow her on Twitter @NancyMarmolejo

Public relations as we know it has been turned on its ear with the advent of social networking. As any PR person can tell you, the majority of publicity and media leads come from good old fashioned relationship building. A 5 minute phone call can do more than 10 well written press releases when you have the right kind of relationship with others.

Twitter provides a perfect environment to cultivate those key relationships with others who can sing your glories, whether they're media contacts or fellow entrepreneurs. The fish-bowl nature of the site enables others to observe your news-worthiness simply by following you.

As you're traversing the Twitterverse, remember that you're not communicating in a vacuum. People are watching you and learning about you from your actions, your posts, and how you present yourself.

Now more than ever is the time to focus on your approachability quotient. When you show up as an approachable member of the Twitterverse, you're presenting yourself as an easy to connect with person, and those connections can lead to free PR, lucrative JV offers, and lots of great publicity.

Take this list of questions and hold it up against your Twitter streams and your overall presence. From your quick little profile to your individual Tweets, look for alignment and make a few tweaks if necessary.

Does your Twitter profile "smile"?

Besides a nice photo of yourself, is the language and wording on your profile friendly? A good exercise is to actually SMILE as you write. Seriously, give that a try when you update your profile and see what words flow from you. You only have a short amount of words to use, but make them work for you.

What does your profile photo say?

A picture speaks a thousand words, and with the quantum power of social networking, your photo is going to be seen by a lot of people! Whether you want something relaxed or posed, it's important to understand the energy your profile photo is conveying. Use a close-up shot for best results- remember, the actual profile image is going to be quite small and anything farther away than a close up won't be seen well.

Are your comments projecting a positive or negative attitude?

How you break the ice with others will set the tone for how people perceive you. If your habit is to complain, then that's what you'll get known as: a complainer. If you're a person who spots the positive and shares with others positive things, then that's what you'll get known as. (Hint: go for the positive approach!) It also builds your credibility as an expert and experts are what the media are seeking out when they scan the Twitterverse for leads.

Is everything always about YOU or do you leave space for others?

As wonderful as you are, Twitter is not the place to grandstand or endlessly self-promote. One of the best ways to raise your approachability quotient is to step out and put the focus away from yourself. Follow my Golden Rule of Twitter: Tweet unto others 10 times more than you Tweet unto yourself.

Do you balance the personal and the professional?

One of my "magic secrets" to social networking is to balance the personal and professional. Let's use an offline example to illustrate this one: the golf course. People have been doing business on the golf course for ages, but how does it happen? Well, I hope this doesn't come as too big a surprise but folks aren't going straight to talking business out there! After checking in how the last vacation was, how that remodel project is coming along, what club they're going to use on the next shot, then the skilled schmoozer slips in some business talk-well timed and well balanced. You want to find that balance in both the information you put out there and the communication you strike up with others.

When you focus on making yourself more approachable on Twitter, you increase the ability for others to know, like, and trust you. You also increase your approachability, which can lead to lucrative publicity and offers. Look over your activities online and see if you could increase your approachability quotient with these handy tips.

Chapter 23

Trend-Spotting, Mobile Marketing & Smart Mobs

FLASH MOBS

Long before things like social media was the hot buzzword of the day, there were Web forums and newsgroups that served as the primary place where social communication took place.

People would go from forum to forum to spread news about people, products, services they bought or experience, sharing whether it was a good or bad experience.

The overall effect of this type of promotion was usually limited, but it was still possible to get people riled up over something on a much larger scale.

One of the best of the classic **online flash mobs** initiated by the tribe can be seen anytime anyone says something bad about Mac or Apple products.

The moment you post anything you don't like about a Mac, you can almost bet that within minutes you'll get a bunch of @ replies from the Apple Tribe arguing against whatever has been said.

At any moment, I can whine about how my iPhone bugs me, and I'll get a slew of people sending me replies about it. Many are helpful responses from people truly wanting to help fix my problem. Others are true believers of Apple, who can't believe there could possibly be anything bad about a MAC.

When I first got my iPhone, I tweeted my discontent about there being no copy/paste feature. To which an immediate reply from someone in Australia where the iPhone had yet to be sold, saying, "Oh that's got to be impossible! MAC was the first computer to invent the copy/paste feature."

I'm still smiling when I think of the raving fan Apple has in this tweeter. Now THAT's Tribal Seduction at its best!

Government take down Flash Mob powered by SMS
Flash mobs may have started as a form of performance art, most of them "funny pranks" to freak people out in a crowd. But they've evolved to organize more influential movements with political impact.

The first revolutionary flash mob with political consequence was seen in January 2001 when Filipinos took to the streets to force the resignation of their president Joseph Estrada, who appeared to be on the verge of being exonerated after a long trial on charges of corruption.

It's known as the 'People Power II' uprising, and it was powered by SMS to coordinate the protests, keep protestors abreast of events as they unfolded and to mobilize citizens to march and take action as a unified group of people.

Filipinos gathered at one of Manila's major highways, Epifanio de los Santos Avenue. Four days of public protesting coordinated through mobile texting (SMS) was credited with compelling the president to leave office.

The uprising garnered wide media attention in part because mobile phones were launched in the Philippines only three years earlier in 1999. By 2001, texting among Filipinos was being described as the 'national pastime' according to Bella

Ellwood-Clayton in 'Texting and God: The Lord is My Textmate—Folk Catholicism in the Cyber Philippines' (2003).

Smart Mobs

While Twitter may be a new form of personal broadcasting and word-of-mouth marketing in the United States, the concept of SMS and text messaging is not new around the world.

Japanese malls send SMS via Bluetooth technology the instant someone walks through the entrance telling them what stores are having major sales, which helps drive traffic directly to any store they've been monitoring that needs more business.

All a company needs to do is open their mind to the possibilities of how to use Twitter as a form of communicating their message to the masses, and we could continue writing for the next 1,000 pages with all the ideas of different strategies that could be activated.

Howard Rheingold shares in "Smart Mobs – The next social revolution" how "smart mobs consist of people who are able to act in concert even if they don't know each other. The people who make up smart mobs cooperate in ways never before possible because they carry devices that possess both communication and computing capabilities."

Whether it's getting communication out from your government, or organizing people to get the message TO your government, Twitter and other micro-blogging, SMS tools can be used in an infinite number of powerful ways.

Beyond business. Beyond politics. Twitter is just the beginning.

Mobile marketing is the wave of the future. It's here now for early adopters.

Whether it's to raise money for a worth-while charity or raise awareness on an important issue, Twitter is changing the way we do business and market online.

The only question now is, **how will YOU apply the technology to make an impact in your world?**

Chapter 24

Twitter is Like Sex

Now that you've read all about how to Tweet, what to tweet, and the ins and outs of Twitter, including why micro-blogging has become all the rage; the time has come for you to spread your wings, jump out of the nest, and fly. Try it on for yourself. It's not easily explained, and it means so many different things to different people. But once you really "get it" you'll be like every other convert—ADDICTED and wondering how you ever communicated without it!

The bottom line is you've got to experience it for yourself.

The best way to illustrate this point was perfectly described in an article I read on a new friend's blog that I met on Twitter *@Remarkablogger http://remarkablogger.com*

Twitter is like sex.
Contributed with permission by @Remarkablogger

Twitter is like sex. You can read all the stuff (or look at it) about sex all you want, but if you've never had it, you simply have no idea what it's like.

And once you've had sex, you know you could never hope to really explain it to someone else. You will sound like a complete idiot if you try. If you're trying to explain it to your kid, you will sound even worse than an idiot, but that's another matter entirely.

Twitter is the same way. Saying that you write short missives of less than 140 characters in answer to the question "What are you doing?" except that nobody really answers the question sounds about as awe-inspiring as saying, *"Well, when Mommy and Daddy love each other very much, um... well, there's a ...and a... a... hey, ya' know what, why don't you go ask your mother?"* And even if you manage to describe the mechanics of the act, it doesn't exactly leave your rapt listener with any notion about what all the shouting's about.

This is why I say you just have to give Twitter a try for a couple weeks and there's no way to really explain it.

Sex is not about just getting something from others. You have to give. In fact, giving can be just as good as "getting," right? Twitter is like that (I'm going to uh... pump this analogy for all its worth). If you just show up and say "where're all my opportunities?" you might as well just stay off Twitter. But if you go looking to give to others, you will have plenty of friends and you'll grow your network.

You know that desperate person at the party who will sleep with just about anybody, but nobody ever wants to take them up on it? They're on Twitter, too. You will recognize them by their tweets (that's what you call a post on Twitter, and yes, I know it's silly). Their tweets will consist of only links to their own blog posts. They are following thousands of people, but nobody is following them (instead of "friends," Twitter has "followers"). Stay away from the easy, cheap & sleazy.

Stick with quality. How will you know? They're the people that just about everyone else is following. They're the ones providing value in one form or another: cool links, humorous tidbits, and lively conversation.

Now, I know that not every social media site is for everyone. Twitter is technically micro-blogging, but the social component is its strongest feature. I don't care for Facebook, for example.

Twitter is Like Sex

There's something for everyone. I'm not saying you should be on Twitter if you hate it.

I'm just saying that Twitter is about as explainable as sex is.

For a good time, follow me on Twitter *@Remarkablogger ;)*

PART FOUR

The iChapters

The Twitter Playbook

You'll find these iChapters online in order to keep the information shared in this ever-changing, fast-paced trend of micro-blogging and social networking current and relevant to you the reader, and the community who uses online social networks to grow their business or stay connected with their circle of connections.

This is the part of the book that YOU get the opportunity to write and be a part of history—a part of the Social Media Revolution. You can do this by participating and placing comments or resources, updates and anything relevant to the topic.

iChapters are designed to be interactive chapters where the community contributes to and adds their brilliance, resources, and expertise. Join us and add YOUR two cents. Or as we say in twitter-style, your 140 worth!

Do that now by visiting the following links on the online book at: http://TwitterHandbook.com

Chapters 25 - 32

25. Twinterviews
http://Twinterviews.com

26. Twitter Videos (How-to & Influencers)
http://TwitterHandbook.com/blog/videos

27. FAQ's
http://TwitterHandbook.com/blog/FAQ

28. TwitCastRadio (weekly / monthly shows)
http://TwitCastRadio.com

29. Twitter Apps (updated)
http://TwitterHandbook.com/blog/apps

30. Future of Twitter & Twitter Alternatives
http://TwitterHandbook.com/blog/future

31. Glossary of terms for Twitter (expanded)
http://TwitterHandbook.com/blog/glossary

Chapter 32

The Final Chapter

Do not read this Chapter.

It's for our own justification purposes to our business partners that we're writing this book about Twitter, micro-blogging, social networks, and mobile communications for "business reasons."

Truth be told, Warren and I are both addicts. Twaddicts. We enjoy interacting and learning from all types of people on Twitter. Quite frankly, our lives are better for it. We confess only to some that when Twitter is down, we're not happy.

But we get excited to see all the programmers rising to the surface to create products to serve a similar role as Twitter— just on different, private networks. We look forward to all the exciting new developments that are on the horizon of this new Social Media Revolution.

And we're thrilled to meet you and others who are taking the journey with us.

Please don't tell my business partner @JPmicek that I'm on Twitter for the fun of it! Instead, tell him you loved THIS chapter the best—even though we don't even want you to read it—because it's shameless self-promotion of what we're all about in our business lives, and what both Warren and I do for a living apart from partnering together on this project, that allows me to live in Hawaii and Warren to live in Vegas—the conference capitol of the nation.

This way we can justify the business and marketing aspects of investing hundreds of hours researching and writing this book.

Deal?

About the Authors

Warren Whitlock
@WarrenWhitlock

Warren Whitlock is a #1 best selling author, publisher, and editor of the BestSellerAuthors.com blog focused on book marketing.

Warren has been an entrepreneur in the computer and imaging industries, several offline businesses and Internet properties. He started his career in broadcast advertising, developing cross promotions between two or more businesses, and has used the same strategies in direct mail and now online and social media.

Over the past decade, Warren has taught thousands of small businesses, authors and individuals how to use proven direct marketing principles to promote their products and services. He's started a trade association, served on several executive boards and teaches social media marketing.

Warren offers a FREE course for authors (or anyone who wants to be known on the net as an expert) at

http://BookMarketingStrategy.com

And when he's not doing all of the above... he's tweeting. Follow him http://twitter.com/warrenwhitlock

Warren Whitlock
Book Marketing Strategist
http://BestSellerAuthors.com

Facebook: http://warrenwhitlock.com/facebook
Blog: http://BestSellerAuthors.com/blog

About the Authors

Deborah Micek (AKA: Coach Deb) Speaker's Bio:

Featured in the Wall Street Journal, columnist for **Entrepreneur** Magazine and **Honolulu Star Bulletin**, radio show guest for the TV reality series *The Apprentice*, and life coach for the award winning TV reality show *Dream Makeover Hawaii*, getting free publicity has become a specialty for **Deborah Micek**, the highly sought after new media marketing consultant.

Author of the first published book on New Media Marketing, *Secrets of Online Persuasion*, Coach Deb ranks among bleeding edge experts and trendsetters—all while keeping things simple for her clients.

With her degree in psychology, Deborah started RPM Success Group ® Inc. as her first consultancy company in the year 2000 with her partner John-Paul Micek after running and selling several multi-million dollar companies. RPM Success Group ® Inc. became the only coaching company focused on the science of persuasion for small business owners to grow their business and the psychology of building your brand from the inside out.

Co-creator of the **world's premiere new media marketing software system**, **Blogi360.com**, Coach Deb gave her clients the unfair advantage to level the playing field with large corporations with big budgets. Now, Coach Deb is living the ultimate business owner's lifestyle; leveraging new media to work with clients from 13 countries—all from the most remote island chain in the world. Enjoying life in tropical paradise on the island of Oahu is a dream come true for Coach Deb.

Sit up tall and get ready to participate, because this is one Coach whose energy is contagious!

Review her credentials at: http://DeborahMicek.com

Subscribe to Coach Deb's blog at: http://TribalSeduction.com

Tap into her auto-pilot marketing system at: http://Blogi360.com

What Coach Deb's been up to these days:

Her latest coaching course, Tribal Seduction, has become the talk of top persuasion and influence gurus for its revolutionary strategies on marketing and influence in the 21st Century.

The *Twitter Handbook* is her current community project with Warren Whitlock, getting buzz everywhere from the internet marketing community to the blogosphere; all a result of the innovative new media marketing strategies she's launched, setting the trend of how products will be created, bought, and sold in the 21st Century.

Deborah is most famous for creating Blogi360.com with her partner and team of programmers. This system goes much further than a traditional website or blog. It's become the new media marketing hub for small business owners to attract and convert a loyal tribe of clients who buy again and again. Sales and social marketing are put on auto-pilot with this system, giving business owners more free time to do the things they love.

****

Connect with Coach Deb by following her on Twitter: http://Twitter.com/CoachDeb or tuning into her new TV show http://iDebi.TV

The BEST place to keep in touch with Coach Deb is to subscribe to her most active blog and get FREE coaching, tips, and bleeding edge resources before it's even tweeted: http://TribalSeduction.com

Get her book *Secrets of Online Persuasion* in your local bookstore or direct from Amazon: http://snipurl.com/SOPhardcover

Check out the only website that works FOR you and puts sales and social marketing on auto-pilot for $1.00 trial (Limited Time Offer) http://Blogi360.com

Thanks for reading this copy of The Twitter Revolution.

We trust you enjoyed reading it as much as we enjoyed putting it all together with the help of the Twitterverse.

Please share your feedback and tell us what your favorite part of this comprehensive, hands-on guide to all things Twitter and new media marketing by sending us an @ reply on Twitter so we can get to know you.

Send your feedback to:

@CoachDeb and @WarrenWhitlock

You can also share your comments/feedback/review/endorsement on this book so others may learn from it and join the social media revolution by leaving a blog comment on:

http://TwitterHandbook.com/blog/book

Deborah Micek and Warren Whitlock

See ya' on Twitter